# Embroidering Life

## Stitching Patterns and Projects
## for Every Season

### Yumiko Higuchi

# Contents

Note: Any and all of the projects included in this book are prohibited from commercial use or sale. Please enjoy handcrafting them for your own purposes.

# Introduction

This book is called *Embroidering Life* because it's chock-full of seasonal motifs that we see all around us in our day-to-day lives, as well as special events and excursions, and the delicious foods and fun times we have.

The inspiration for the book is a series, Everyday Stitches, which previously appeared in Bunka Publishing Bureau's women's magazine, *Misesu*. I updated and expanded those patterns as I created the contents included here.

My mother loved reading *Misesu*, which was in print from September 1961 through April 2021. I myself found it to be an impressive publication, every issue filled with admirable people, places, and things, shown in beautiful photographs with lovely styling and thoughtful captions and features.

Although that series only lasted for one year and four months, it was a very fulfilling experience. I'll always be grateful for the efforts that went into producing it and I have deeply fond memories of the entire process. Returning to the projects here, I fell in love with these stitches all over again, losing myself in re-creating them.

The patterns here come straight from my heart. In these troubling times of ongoing disease, strife, and hardship, I gathered together designs that depict a relaxing lifestyle. I had fun arranging them—it was like playing house, creating playful shapes and colors that convey a heartwarming atmosphere, filled with cherished motifs and images that conjure joyful celebrations over the months of the year.

Everyday life brims with inspiration, and my hopes and dreams, along with the desire to create, are boundless. I hope to continue stitching, designing patterns imbued with the rich charm and sense of beauty in everyday things that I learned from the pages of *Misesu*.

*—Yumiko Higuchi*

## Kadomatsu | page 64

Traditional Japanese pine decorations to welcome the New Year play
well with hardy little flowers that bloom in the snow. Celebrate the New
Year with an auspicious design that will bring good fortune.

## Japanese New Year's Decorations | pages 70, 99

Pine, bamboo, rice, plum, daidai orange, urajiro fern, false daphne, nandina: these are the plants and flowers that bring good luck and summon the spirit of a new year. Here they're arranged on your embroidery hoop to create a festive *shimekazari* wreath.

*Adonis Ramosa* | page 71

Snowball Fight | page 72

## Camellias | Page 64

As the snow begins to melt, we can hear birds chirping, signaling the coming
spring. February is also the month for Valentine's Day, which stirs the heart.

Birds Singing in Spring | page 73

Bouquet of Tulips │ page 74

Baking Sweets | page 75

MARCH

## Cherry Tree | page 65

Cherry blossoms are lovely in full bloom as well as when
their petals scatter. The drama of this fleeting moment is
memorable as we celebrate spring's arrival.

Hinamatsuri—Girls' Day | page 76

Violet Garden | page 74

## Violet Sachet | pages 74, 99

Violets are so sweet with their delicately hued flowers. Fill this sachet with
your favorite scent to make a delightful gift. It can even be sewn by hand.

APRIL

## Herb Flowers | page 65

Gardening for Easter, it's also a time to prepare for spring.
Despite the busyness of spring, the buds and sprouts of so
many plants and flowers are a welcome sight.

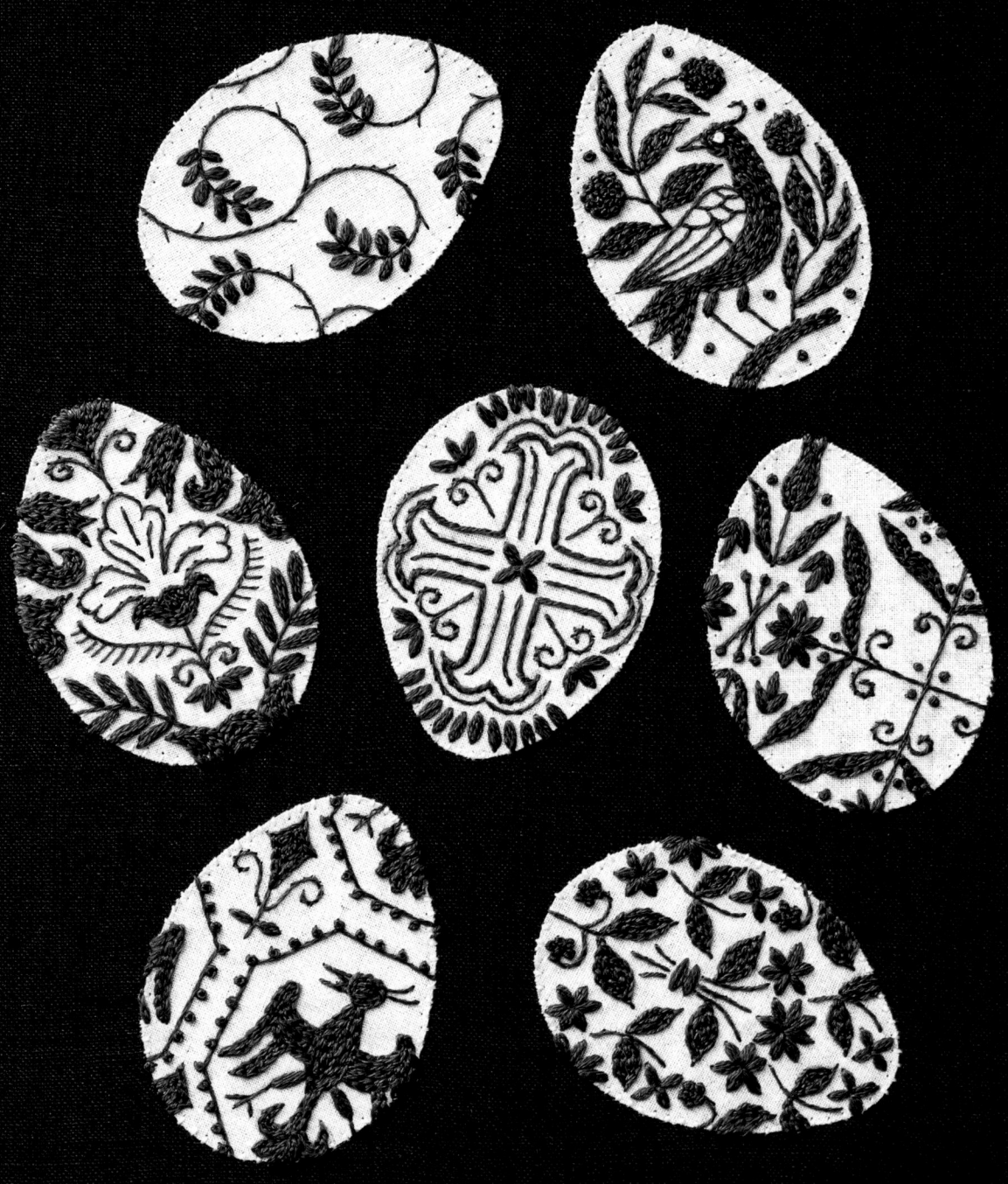

Easter Eggs │ page 77

Gardening | page 78

Stationery | page 79

## Bonsai Plant | page 66

It's such a pleasant season when spring's greenery is fresh and beautiful. May is also an excellent time to plan events or to travel.

Travel | page 80

Spring Wreath | page 81

## Koinobori (Carp Streamer) Tapestry | pages 82, 100

May 5 is Children's Day in Japan. The holiday promotes happiness and well-being for all children. Why not make a tapestry streamer to use as a festive decoration?

## Lily of the Valley and Hydrangea | page 66

June is the rainy season in Japan. Have fun indoors with these lovely designs
featuring teatime and the lush blooms and verdure that emerge with so much rain.

Passionflower Wreath | page 83

Wedding | page 84

## Teatime | pages 85, 100

This design depicts a secret teatime scene in the forest. Embroider
delicious desserts in a repeating pattern on this delightful fabric panel.

## Tanabata | page 67

The Star Festival on July 7 means that summer has arrived. Tanabata
is the first of many traditional summer festivals in Japan. A festive
cocktail tastes even better when enjoyed under a starry sky.

Cocktails / Page 86

Cactus Pattern | page 87

Blue Flowers in Summer | pages 87, 99

Balloon flowers, shaggy dwarf morning glories, and tweedia milkweed—summer's blue-petaled blooms are packed tightly in this petite hoop pattern. You can feel the refreshing breeze.

## Hibiscus | page 67

August's heat can be relentless. Taking advantage of the foods in season can shore up your body's defenses against summer fatigue. The colorful motifs of the coral and summer vegetables in the following designs are fun to stitch.

Coral Forest | page 88

Summer Foods | page 89

## Triangular Pot Holder | pages 89, 101

This adorable pot holder with a lobster icon looks like a
triangular hat. It makes it easy to grab a hot pot handle.

SEPTEMBER

## Harvest Moon Viewing | page 68

As summer's heat recedes, the occasional breeze carries with
it signs of autumn. The night is filled with the sound of insects,
and we delight in the lingering plants and flowers.

Seven Flowers of Autumn | page 90

## Lesson Bag | pages 101, 103

Stitch your favorite instrument with the word *lesson* onto a simple tote bag. This tote
is big enough for oversized music books and sheet music to fit conveniently inside.

*Osmanthus* | page 68

Autumn is the season of bountiful harvest. Gathered together here are designs featuring plants, fruits, and vegetables in a warm array of colors.

Pumpkin Patch | page 92

Pear Pattern | pages 93, 100

This pattern showcases ripe pears in an elegant color scheme. Work it as a fabric panel and it lends warmth to any room.

## Cosmos | page 69

As we get deeper into the season, the north wind blows
and the trees gradually change color. Autumn is the
perfect time for cozy hours at home, reading and knitting.

Autumn Wreath | page 94

Cozy Time at Home | page 95

## Book Cover with Fallen Leaves | pages 92, 102

Perfect for autumn reading, this chic book cover features a colorful
arrangement of fallen leaves and chestnuts.

## Christmas Tree Snow Globe | page 69

In the season of falling snow, delight in stitching these Christmas motifs
featuring a snow globe, handknit mittens, and a nutcracker doll.

Handknit Mittens | pages 96

# Ribbon Brooch | pages 97, 102

These accessories are ornamented with a veritable collection of seasonal greenery and berries.

# Christmas Botanical Ring Pillow | page 98, 103

Nutcracker Doll | pages 97, 99

# Tools

A **Cellophane**
Use this material to transfer patterns onto fabric so that the tracing paper doesn't tear.

B **Tracing Paper**
This thin paper is for copying patterns.

C **Chalk Paper**
Use this paper to transfer patterns onto fabric. For dark fabric, use white chalk paper.

D **Tracer**
Use this tool to trace patterns when transferring onto fabric. You can also use a ballpoint pen. Another option is to use a light box. In that case, I recommend using a fine-tipped heat erasable fabric marking pen (see "Transferring Patterns (1)" on page 61).

E **Eyeleteer**
Use this tool for perforations.

F **Embroidery Scissors**
Small, sharp, pointed scissors with a thin edge are the easiest to use.

G **Tailor's Shears**
It's best to have sharp shears that are specifically made for cutting fabric.

H **Needle Threader**
This tool makes it easier to put the thread into the eye of a needle.

I **Needles and Pincushion**
I use French embroidery needles with sharp points. The needle size depends on how many strands of embroidery floss are used.

J **Embroidery Hoops**
Use embroidery hoops to stretch fabric tightly. I recommend the smaller 4" hoop, since it's a comfortable size to hold and work with when stitching. When working with a larger pattern, you may need to slide the hoop over your work. When stretching the fabric in your embroidery hoop, fasten the bracket securely. If your embroidery hoop is fastened too loosely, the fabric can sag and wrinkle. You can also wrap the inner hoop with bias tape or fabric (I recommend using white) to help prevent slippage.

## EMBROIDERY FLOSS

For all the projects in this book, I used No. 25 embroidery floss. Six-stranded floss is the most popular. The brand I use is DMC embroidery floss from France, which is known for its vivid colors and lustrous texture.

## FABRIC

All of the projects here are made using linen. Plain-weave linen is easy to work with, can be washed, and has a smooth texture, so it's perfectly suited for embroidery fabric. It's best to wash linen before cutting it to size, then dry it away from direct sunlight. To readjust the fabric grain, iron the linen lightly before it's completely dry. For the appliqués, I used lightweight cotton fabric, such as batiste; and for *zakka* (small) projects, such as the pot holder, I also used quilt cloth to provide a cushioned lining.

## NUMBER OF STRANDS AND NEEDLE SIZE

Choose the size of your needle based on the number of strands you are using. By doing so, you'll always have the perfect needle for whatever project you're working on. The thickness of the fabric you're using also determines the size.

| NO. 25 EMBROIDERY FLOSS | EMBROIDERY NEEDLE |
|---|---|
| 6 strands | No. 3/4 |
| 3–4 strands | No. 5/6 |
| 1–2 strands | Nos. 7–10 |

*These are standard sizes of Clover needles.

# Basic Stitches

## Straight Stitch

The simplest stitch for needlework. You can produce different effects depending on the direction or length of the stitch, the way you arrange the stitches, or the number of strands you use.

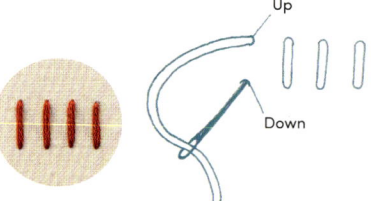

## Running Stitch

This stitch creates a dotted line. Once you get the knack for this stitch, you can really run with it.

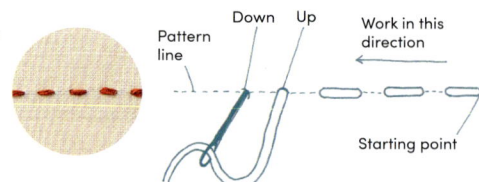

## Backstitch

This stitch gives the appearance of machine stitching. You backstitch with every stitch as your work progresses forward.

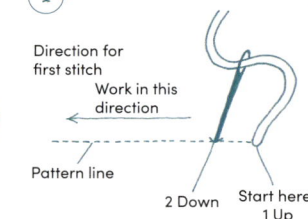

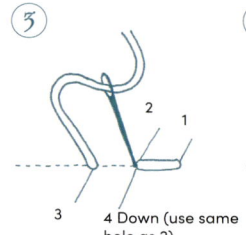

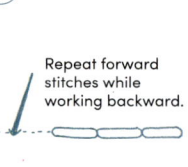

## Outline Stitch

This is the fundamental stitch for creating lines. I often use this for borders and stems on plants and flowers. Adjust the thickness by the number of strands.

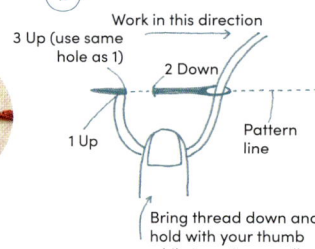

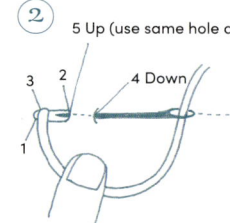

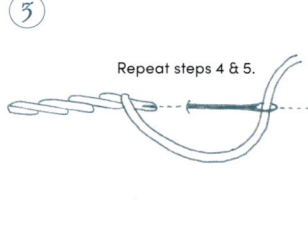

## Chain Stitch

This stitch creates linked loops like a chain. It creates thick lines, or it can be used to fill in areas if you're careful not to leave any gaps.

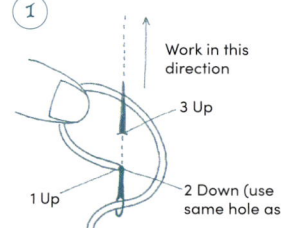

Bring your needle up at 1, form a loop with the thread, and insert it back, using the same hole.

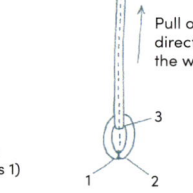

Pull thread out, and slowly tighten until the loop is the desired size.

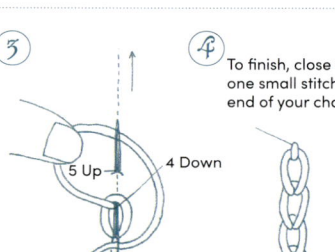

Bring needle down, using same hole as 3, then bring back up one stitch length away. Repeat steps 2 & 3.

## Lazy Daisy Stitch

This is created with a single chain stitch. It's used for small flower petals and leaves. In this book, it's often combined with a straight stitch.

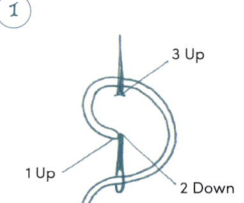

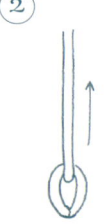

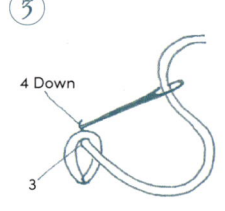

## Lazy Daisy Stitch + Straight Stitch

Sew one or two straight stitches across the center of the lazy daisy to create an oval shape that has volume. Adjust the size depending on the number of strands to use this stitch for various small flower petals, leaves, fruit, and seeds.

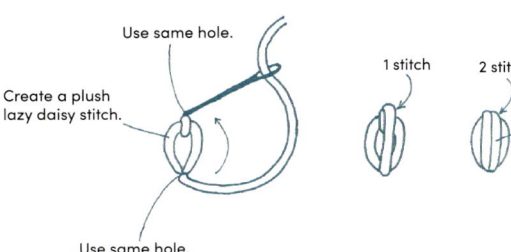

Use same hole.

Create a plush lazy daisy stitch.

Use same hole.

1 stitch

2 stitches

Line up your stitches for a beautiful finish.

## French Knot Stitch

This stitch creates a small knot. The basic French knot stitch is a double wrapage. Adjust the size based on the number of strands of thread. Use them for flower buds and berries, and for animals' eyes. You can also use them to fill in areas. The knots are easily crushed, so work them as you finish a project.

① Bring the needle up at the starting point and wrap thread twice around the tip.

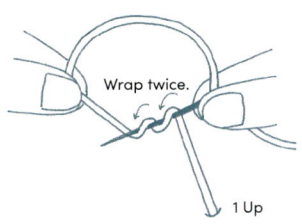

Wrap twice.

1 Up

② Hold the wrapped threads firmly with your finger while inserting the needle at 2.

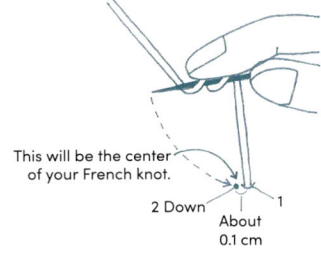

This will be the center of your French knot.

2 Down

About 0.1 cm

**TIP**

If there is a knot on the reverse side, be careful not to get tangled in it.

③ Insert the tip of the needle, hold the needle vertically, and pull the thread tight to the base.

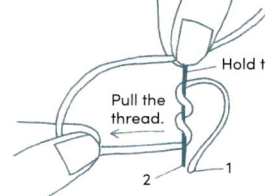

Pull the thread.

Hold the needle vertically.

2    1

④ Hold the thread firmly with your finger while pulling it down through the fabric.

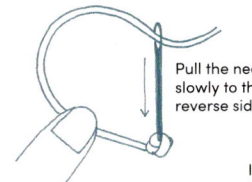

Pull the needle slowly to the reverse side.

If working with coarse fabric, be careful that the knots don't fall through.

## Satin Stitch

Work straight stitches side by side to fill in an area. To create a beautiful finish, line up the parallel threads and make sure they aren't twisted.

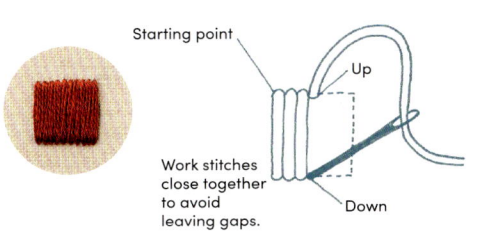

Starting point

Up

Work stitches close together to avoid leaving gaps.

Down

Small Leaf

Starting point

For leaves and such, start at the tip.

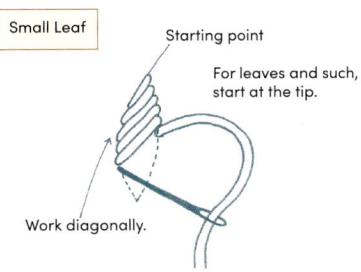

Work diagonally.

## Long and Short Stitch

Long and short stitches are arranged radially toward the center to fill in an area. Use this stitch for things such as fan-shaped flower petals.

① Starting point

Up

Down

Make one stitch at the center, then repeat long and short stitches.

②

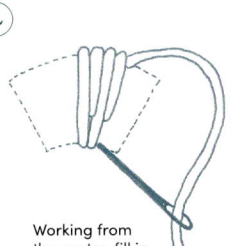

Working from the center, fill in on one side.

③

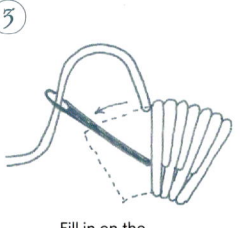

Fill in on the second side.

# Embroidery Techniques

## OUTLINE STITCHES
### Embroider Neat Angles

① Sew outline stitches up to the corner.

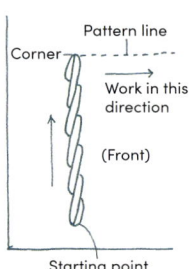

Pattern line

Corner

Work in this direction

(Front)

Starting point

② When you turn the angle, pass the needle through a stitch on the reverse side.

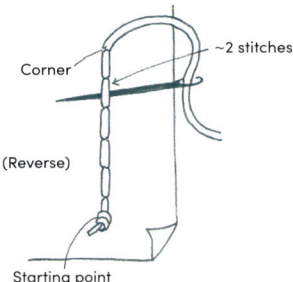

Corner

~2 stitches

(Reverse)

Starting point

③ Bring the needle up at the corner on the front side.

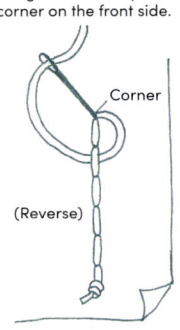

Corner

(Reverse)

④ Continue sewing in the new direction on the right side of the fabric.

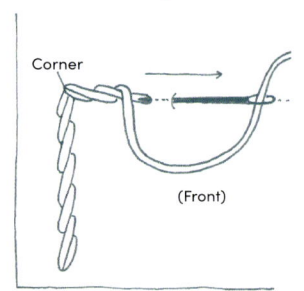

Corner

(Front)

---

## OUTLINE STITCHES
### Embroider Gentle Curves

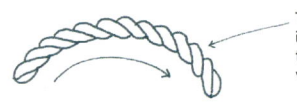

To create an intricate curve, the trick is to make very fine stitches.

## OUTLINE STITCHES
### Embroider Acute Angles

Sew to the tip, using the length of a full stitch to create the point.

Bring the needle up below the stitches, and continue sewing.

---

## CHAIN STITCHES
### Embroider Neat Angles

When you turn the angle, the trick is to sew a bit to the inside, as shown, and continue sewing in the new direction.

## CHAIN STITCHES
### Embroider Acute Angles

Sew to the tip, using the end of a full stitch to create the point.

---

## CHAIN STITCHES
### Embroider Neat Shapes

Pass through

Starting point

Finishing point

When creating a circle or an outline with chain stitches, make sure to connect the first and last stitches for a clean finish.

## CHAIN STITCHES
### Filling In an Area Neatly

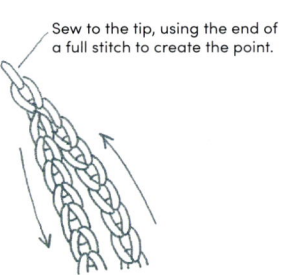

When filling in an area with chain stitches, first sew the outline of the pattern, then sew the additional rows, working from the outside toward the inside. Be careful not to leave any gaps.

**TIP**
If a gap appears, go back at the end and fill in with more outline stitches, which are less noticeable.

**TIP**
For layered stitches, as in the potato at left, work the chain stitches for the base color first.

## SATIN STITCHES
### Techniques for Filling In Areas

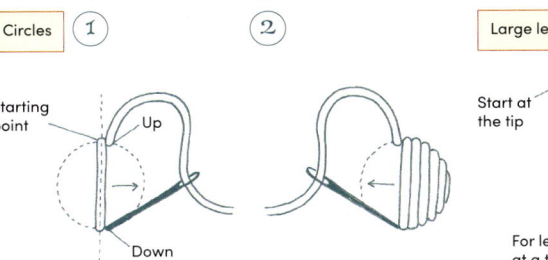

Circles (1) (2)

Starting point
Up
Down

Begin with a first stitch in the center, and then fill in one side.

Fill in the remaining side.

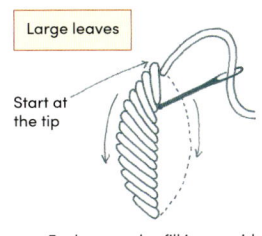

Large leaves

Start at the tip

For leaves, also fill in one side at a time from the center.

*If the leaf has veins, sew the veins first.

## SATIN STITCHES
### Creating More Volume

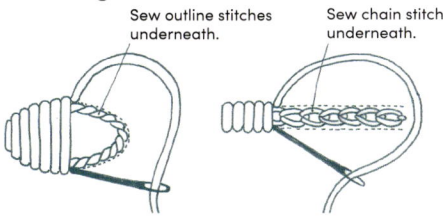

Sew outline stitches underneath.

Sew chain stitches underneath.

Working outline or chain stitches underneath your satin stitches will make your finished work look plush. I recommend this technique for difficult shapes or for beginners and those who dislike satin stitch. When stitching underneath, it's best to use 2 strands in the same color.

## LONG AND SHORT STITCHES
### Techniques for Filling In Areas

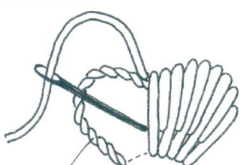

To make three-dimensional — Sew the outline underneath with outline stitches to create a three-dimensional effect.

Sew outline stitches underneath.

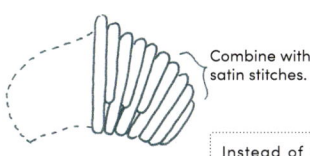

For complicated shapes — For complicated shapes, combine with satin stitches to fill in area.

Combine with satin stitches.

> Instead of using a light box, you can also use a window to see through and transfer your pattern. Use masking tape to affix the tracing paper and fabric from step 1 to a window, and you can see right through it!

## EMBROIDERY FUNDAMENTALS
### Transferring Patterns

First, locate the area where you will transfer the pattern to the fabric. Touch up the fabric with an iron, then arrange the pattern along the warp and weft. Layer (1)–(4) as shown in the photo. Secure with pins, and trace the pattern using a tracer. When using dark-colored fabric, I recommend using white chalk paper.

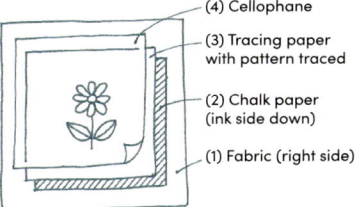

(4) Cellophane

(3) Tracing paper with pattern traced

(2) Chalk paper (ink side down)

(1) Fabric (right side)

### How to Transfer Patterns Using a Light Box

(1) Tracing paper with pattern traced
*If you use a bold-tipped felt pen, it shows up more legibly.

Light box

(2) Fabric (right side)

I recommend using a fine-tipped heat erasable fabric marking pen. The roller-ball-type pens can catch on the fabric, making it difficult to trace.

This can be helpful when transferring large patterns. Layer (1) and (2), and secure with pins. Place face down on top of the light box, and use a heat erasable fabric marking pen to trace the pattern onto the reverse side of the fabric. However, this does not work with thick or dark-colored fabric; in which case, use the fundamental technique on the left.

### Neatening Your Fabric Edge

Neatening your fabric edge will prevent the edges from fraying while embroidering and will make your work go more smoothly. To do so, create a fringed edge on all four sides by gently unraveling the thread for about ¼" on each side, or after completing your work, use pinking shears to cut the fabric.

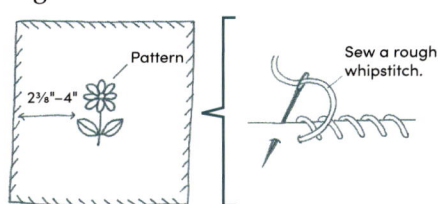

Pattern

2⅜"–4"

Sew a rough whipstitch.

> **TIP**
> The fabric should have a margin of about 2⅜"–4" to allow for being inserted in the embroidery hoop.

## How to Handle Thread

(1)

Pull a standard length of 24" from the skein, and cut the thread.

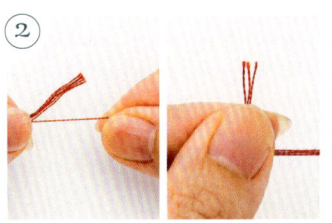

(2)

One at a time, pull the number of strands you need, then arrange them together with the ends aligned neatly.

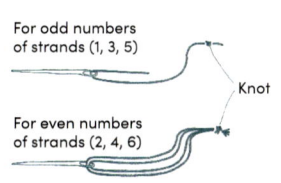

For odd numbers of strands (1, 3, 5)

For even numbers of strands (2, 4, 6)

Knot

For odd numbers of strands, arrange the desired number of strands, thread the needle, and make a knot at one end. For even numbers of strands, thread half the desired number of strands (for 4 strands, thread 2 strands) through the needle, fold it in half and align the ends, and then make a knot.

## Starting Your Embroidery

1. Thread the strands through the needle; place the end of the thread near the tip of the needle.

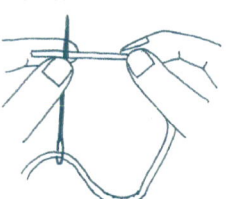

2. Wrap the thread twice around the tip of the needle.

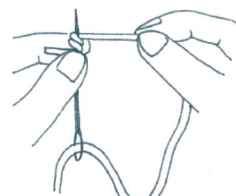

3. Pinch the wrapped thread between your fingertips, slide it down the needle, and pull the knot all the way to the end of the thread.

Slide and pull.

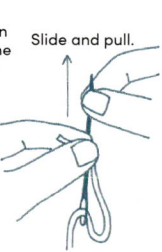

4.

## Finishing Your Embroidery

1. Anchor the thread once you've finished your stitches. Bring the needle up on the reverse side, place the needle through the base of the last stitch, and hold it with your fingers.

Fabric (reverse side)

Embroidery hoop

Last stitch

Press down with your thumb and index finger with the fabric and needle in between.

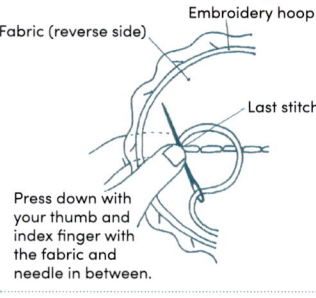

2. Wrap the thread twice around the tip of the needle.

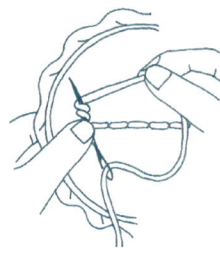

3. Pinch the wrapped thread between your fingertips, and slide it down the needle.

Slide and pull.

Press down tightly.

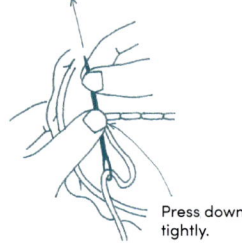

4. Cut the end of the thread.

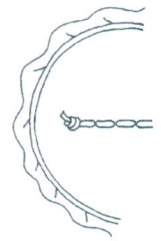

## Starting and Finishing Your Embroidery Cleanly on the Reverse Side

As your embroidery skills improve, you can learn how to neaten up the reverse side too.

**Lines [using chain or outline stitches]**

Start

1. Work a few pick stitches along a line toward the starting point, then bring the needle up at the starting point.

(Front)

Work in this direction

Knot.

Starting point

Pattern line

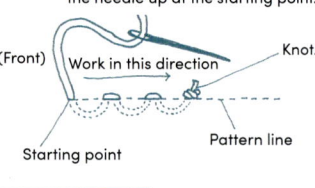

2. Continue working, covering the stitches from step 1.

(Front)

When you reach the knot, clip it off.

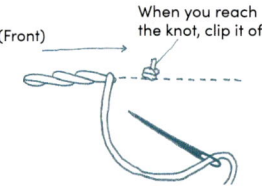

Finish

(Reverse)

Ending point

Existing stitches

Trim excess thread.

When finished, bring the needle up on the reverse side, and anchor the thread by wrapping it through several times around a stitch on this side.

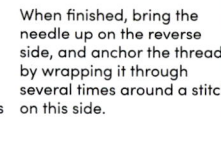

**Filled-in areas using satin stitches**

Start

1. Work a few pick stitches in a line toward the starting point, then bring the needle up at the starting point.

Starting point

Knot.

(Front)

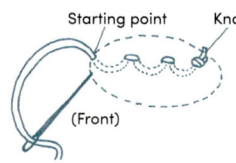

2. Continue working, covering the stitches from step 1.

(Front)

When you reach the knot, clip it off.

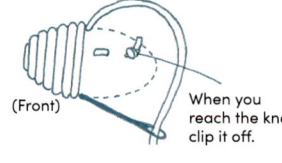

Finish

1. 

(Reverse)

Bring the needle up on the reverse side, and pass the thread under the stitches.

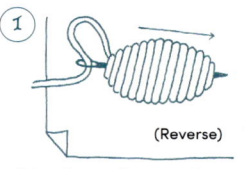

2. 

(Reverse)

Pass the needle back again in the opposite direction, skipping over the first and last few stitches to anchor the thread, and trim excess thread.

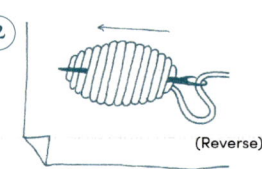

## When Switching Thread

When you run out of thread or need to switch colors, or when working a stem that branches off, start a new thread where stitches already exist by weaving a knotted length of thread around the stitches on the reverse side.

Clip knot later.

(Reverse)

Existing stitches

New starting point

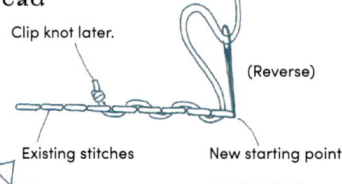

# Embroidery Patterns and Zakka Project Instructions

*The number in parentheses is the number of strands, followed by the color code or name for the DMC No. 25 embroidery floss.

*Unless noted otherwise, all numbers in the project instructions refer to inches.

## Completing Your Project

1. Erase any pattern traces.

   If the marks are water-soluble, mist water on the reverse side of the fabric, then erase any traces that stick out. Use a moistened cotton swab for tight areas.

2. Touch up with an iron.

   Use an iron on the reverse side to lightly touch up any wrinkles. Textural stitches are easily damaged, so spread a towel under the project first. Be careful—once ironed, any traces of the ink will become permanent!

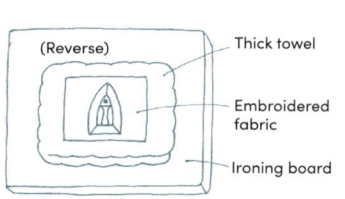

(Reverse) — Thick towel

Embroidered fabric

Ironing board

## U-Shaped Ladder Stitch

For zakka projects, this stitch is used to close the opening for turning out because it creates an invisible seam.

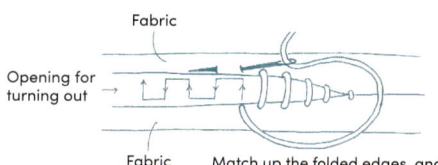

Fabric

Opening for turning out

Fabric

Match up the folded edges, and sew the edges together, creating a U shape.

# MONTHLY EMBLEMS

## Kadomatsu | page 6

*DMC No. 25 embroidery floss: 223, 310, 738, 829, 986, 3052
*Work outline stitch, unless noted otherwise.
*Use 2 strands, unless noted otherwise.
*The number in parentheses is the number of strands, followed by the color code or name for the DMC No. 25 embroidery floss.

(4) 738

Chain 829

Satin (4) From left: 986, 3052, 986

310

French knot (6) 223

Work French knots 738 over chain stitches.

(4) 310

829

Chain 223

French knot (4) 986

Straight (4) 3052

Straight (4) 310

JANUARY

3052

Lazy daisy + straight (4) 986

(4) 738

Work 829 over outline stitches.

Back 310

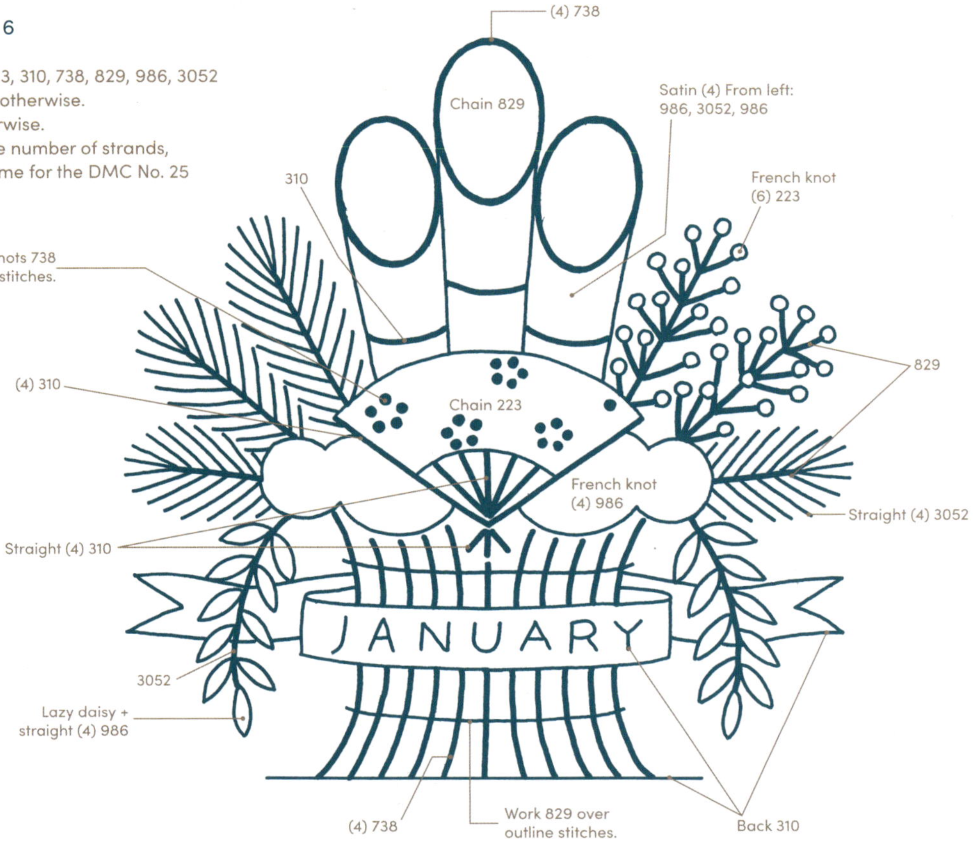

## Camellias | page 10

*DMC No. 25 embroidery floss: 22, 310, 319, 610, 832, 834, 3842, 3865
*Work outline stitch (2 strands) for thick lines.
*Work satin stitch, unless noted otherwise.
*The number in parentheses is the number of strands, followed by the color code or name for the DMC No. 25 embroidery floss.

Long and short (6) 22

French knot (4) 834

832

610

Chain (2) 3865

610

319

From left: 3842, 3865 (alternating)

3842

Chain (2) 3865

3865

FEBRUARY

Back (2) 310

## Cherry Tree | page 14

*DMC No. 25 embroidery floss: 310, 819 (2 skeins), 844, 3354 (2 skeins)
*The number in parentheses is the number of strands, followed by the color code or name for the DMC No. 25 embroidery floss.

French knot (4) Work with 819 & 3354, 2 strands each, threaded onto the same needle.

MARCH

Chain (2) 844

Back (2) 310

## Herb Flowers | page 18

*DMC No. 25 embroidery floss: 32, 310, 320, 470, 632, 699, 987, 3772, 3865
*Work outline stitch (2) 320 for all stems.
*Work satin stitch (4), unless noted otherwise.
*Use 4 strands, unless noted otherwise.
*The number in parentheses is the number of strands, followed by the color code or name for the DMC No. 25 embroidery floss.

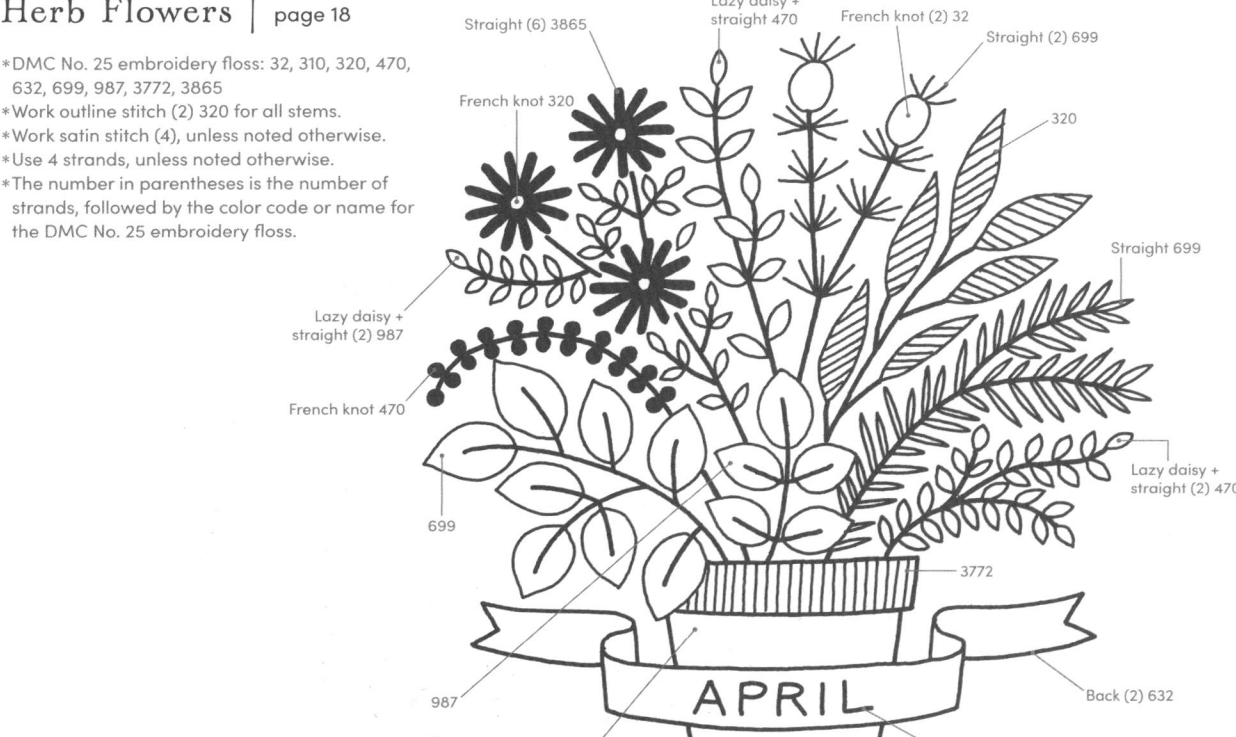

Straight (6) 3865

Lazy daisy + straight 470

French knot (2) 32

Straight (2) 699

French knot 320

320

Lazy daisy + straight (2) 987

Straight 699

French knot 470

Lazy daisy + straight (2) 470

699

3772

987

APRIL

Back (2) 632

Chain (2) 632

Back (2) 310

## Bonsai Plant | page 22

*DMC No. 25 embroidery floss: 501 (2 skeins), 824, 3371, 3790, 3865
*Work chain stitch (2 strands), unless noted otherwise.
*Use 2 strands, unless noted otherwise.
*The number in parentheses is the number of strands, followed by the color code or name for the DMC No. 25 embroidery floss.

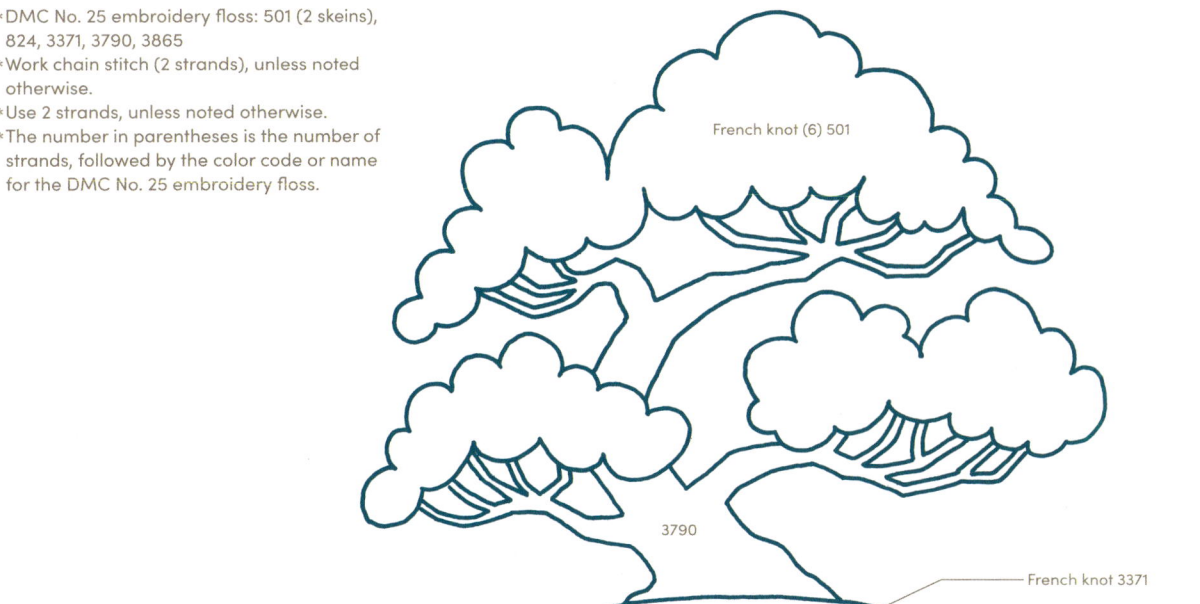

French knot (6) 501

3790

French knot 3371

Outline 824

3865

824

MAY

Work straight stitches 3865 over chain stitches.

Satin (4) 824

## Lily of the Valley and Hydrangea | page 26

*DMC No. 25 embroidery floss: 310, 318, 895, 3346, 3750, 3865
*Use 6 strands, unless noted otherwise.
*The number in parentheses is the number of strands, followed by the color code or name for the DMC No. 25 embroidery floss.

Lazy daisy + straight 3865

Satin 895

Outline (2) 3346

Chain (4) 3750

French knot 3865

JUNE

Lazy daisy + straight 895

Lazy daisy + straight 318

Chain (2) 3750

Back (2) 310

# Tanabata | page 30

*DMC No. 25 embroidery floss: 18, 310, 800, 826, 962, 3350, 3813, 3818
*Work French knots (4 strands) to fill in circles of all sizes.
*Work satin stitch (4 strands) for *tanzaku* (long rectangular strips), unless noted otherwise.
*For all other stitches, work outline stitch (2 strands), unless noted otherwise.
*The number in parentheses is the number of strands, followed by the color code or name for the DMC No. 25 embroidery floss.

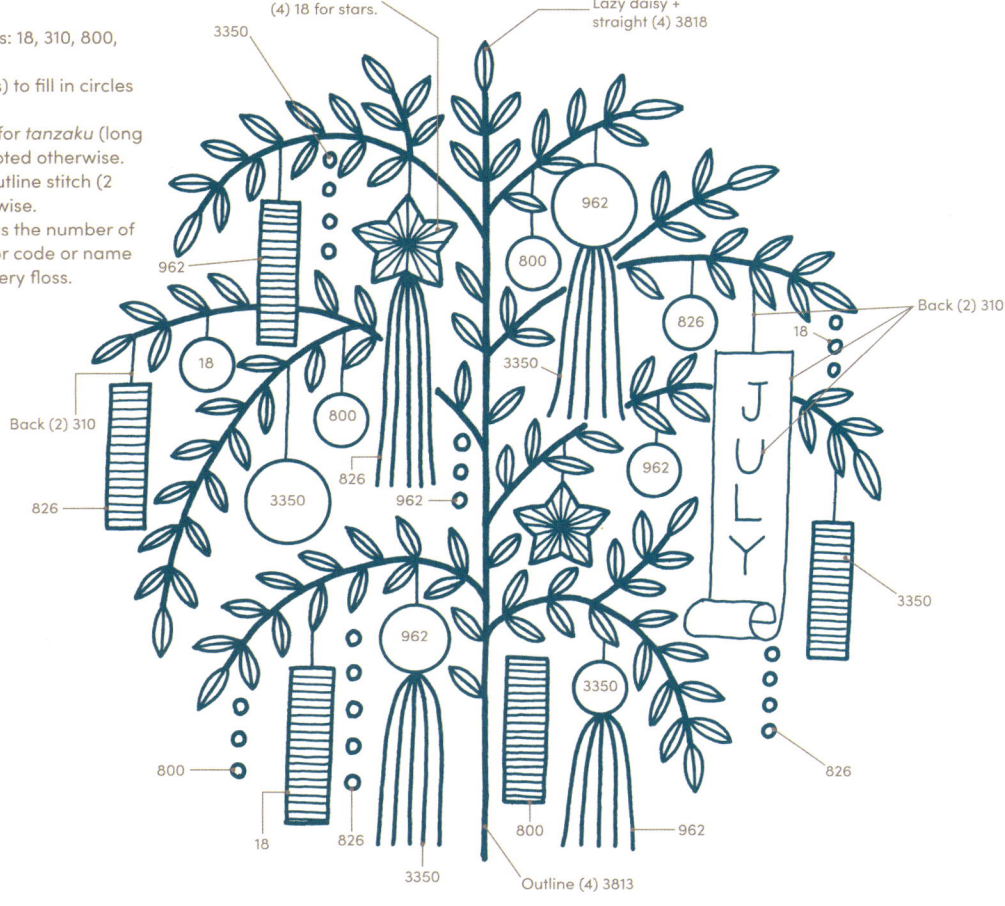

# Hibiscus | page 36

*DMC No. 25 embroidery floss: 225, 310, 321, 600, 677, 931, 961, 988, 3818
*Work long and short stitches (4 strands) for flower petals.
*Use 2 strands, unless noted otherwise.
*The number in parentheses is the number of strands, followed by the color code or name for the DMC No. 25 embroidery floss.

67

# Harvest Moon Viewing | page 40

*DMC No. 25 embroidery floss: 169, 310, 319,
  610, 612, 833, 3865
*Work chain stitch (2 strands), unless noted
  otherwise.
*Use 2 strands, unless noted otherwise.
*The number in parentheses is the number of
  strands, followed by the color code or name
  for the DMC No. 25 embroidery floss.

Satin (4) 169

833

French knot 612

Outline 612

Satin (6) 3865

319

Outline (4) 169

169

319

SEPTEMBER

Back 310

610

310

## *Osmanthus* | page 44

*DMC No. 25 embroidery floss: 310, 520, 838,
  890, 919, 921, 3862
*Use 2 strands, unless noted otherwise.
*The number in parentheses is the number
  of strands, followed by the color code or
  name for the DMC No. 25 embroidery floss.

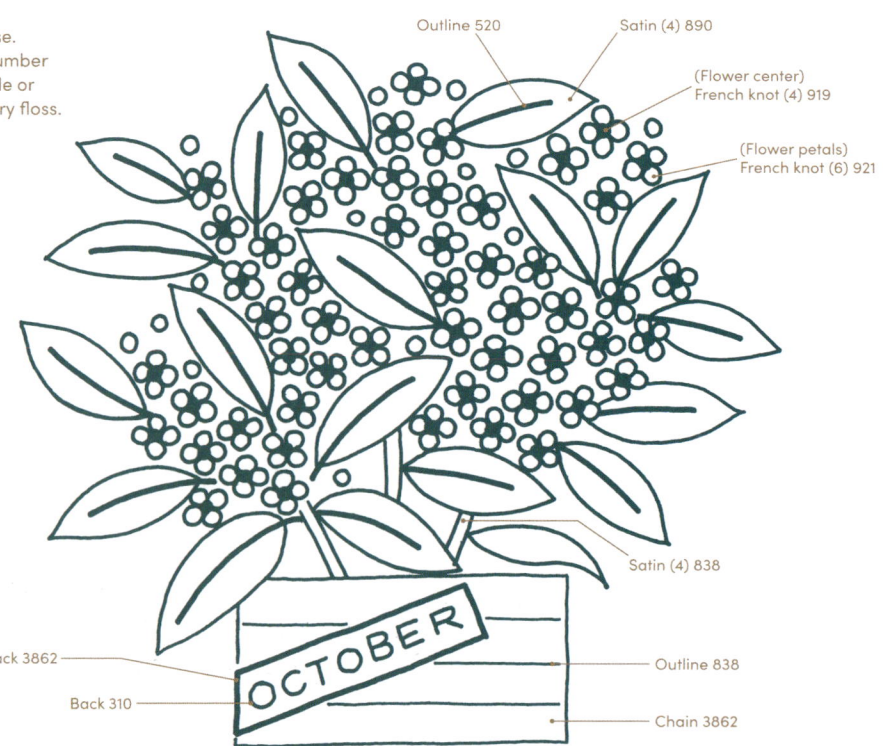

Outline 520

Satin (4) 890

(Flower center)
French knot (4) 919

(Flower petals)
French knot (6) 921

Satin (4) 838

Back 3862

Back 310

OCTOBER

Outline 838

Chain 3862

# Cosmos | page 48

*DMC No. 25 embroidery floss: ecru, 08, 310, 315, 316, 902, 3362, 3364
*Work lazy daisy + straight stitches (4 strands) for flower petals.
*Use 2 strands, unless noted otherwise.
*The number in parentheses is the number of strands, followed by the color code or name for the DMC No. 25 embroidery floss.

315

316

902

(Thick lines) Outline 3364

Outline (1) 3362

(Flower center) Work 4 French knots (4) in ecru.

Chain 08

NOVEMBER

Back 08

Back 310

# Christmas Tree Snow Globe | page 52

*DMC No. 25 embroidery floss: 319, 535, 733, 817, 3866
*Use 2 strands, unless noted otherwise.
*The number in parentheses is the number of strands, followed by the color code or name for the DMC No. 25 embroidery floss.

Straight 733

Outline (4) 3866

Outline 3866

French knot (4) 3866

Straight (4) 319

Outline 319

French knot 3866

French knot (6) 817

Satin (6) 535

Back 535

DECEMBER

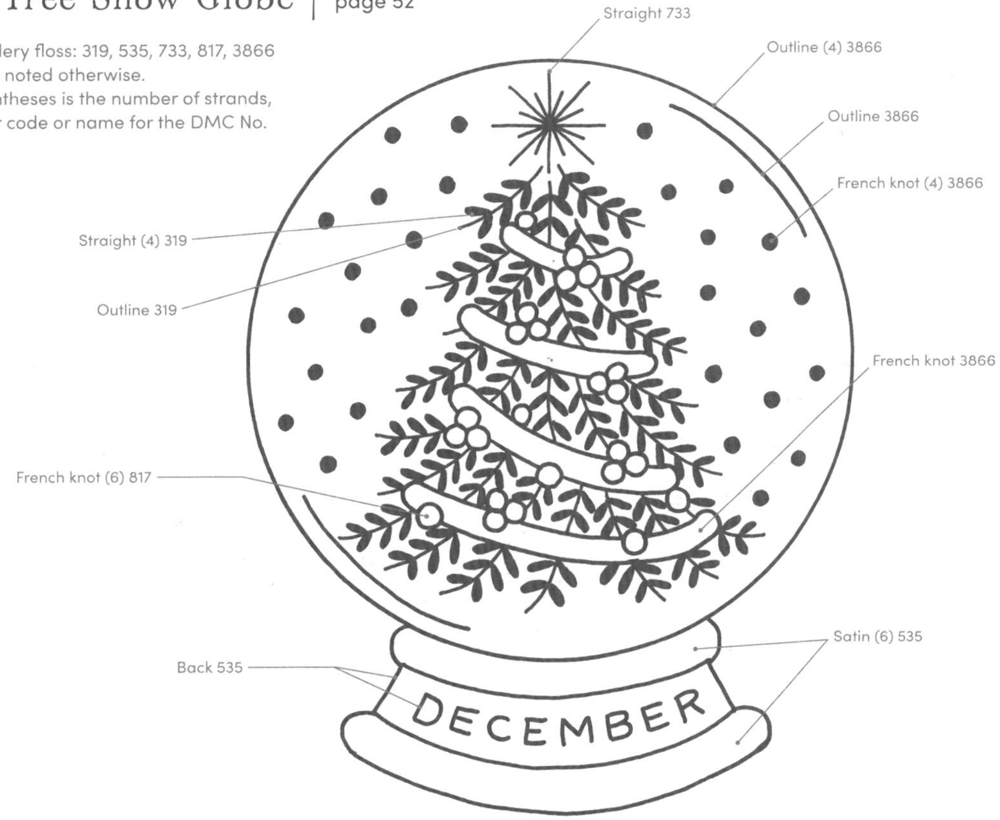

*DMC No. 25 embroidery floss: 22, 610, 612, 976, 3818, 3866
*Work chain stitch (2 strands), unless noted otherwise.
*Use 2 strands, unless noted otherwise.
*The number in parentheses is the number of strands, followed
  by the color code or name for the DMC No. 25 embroidery floss.

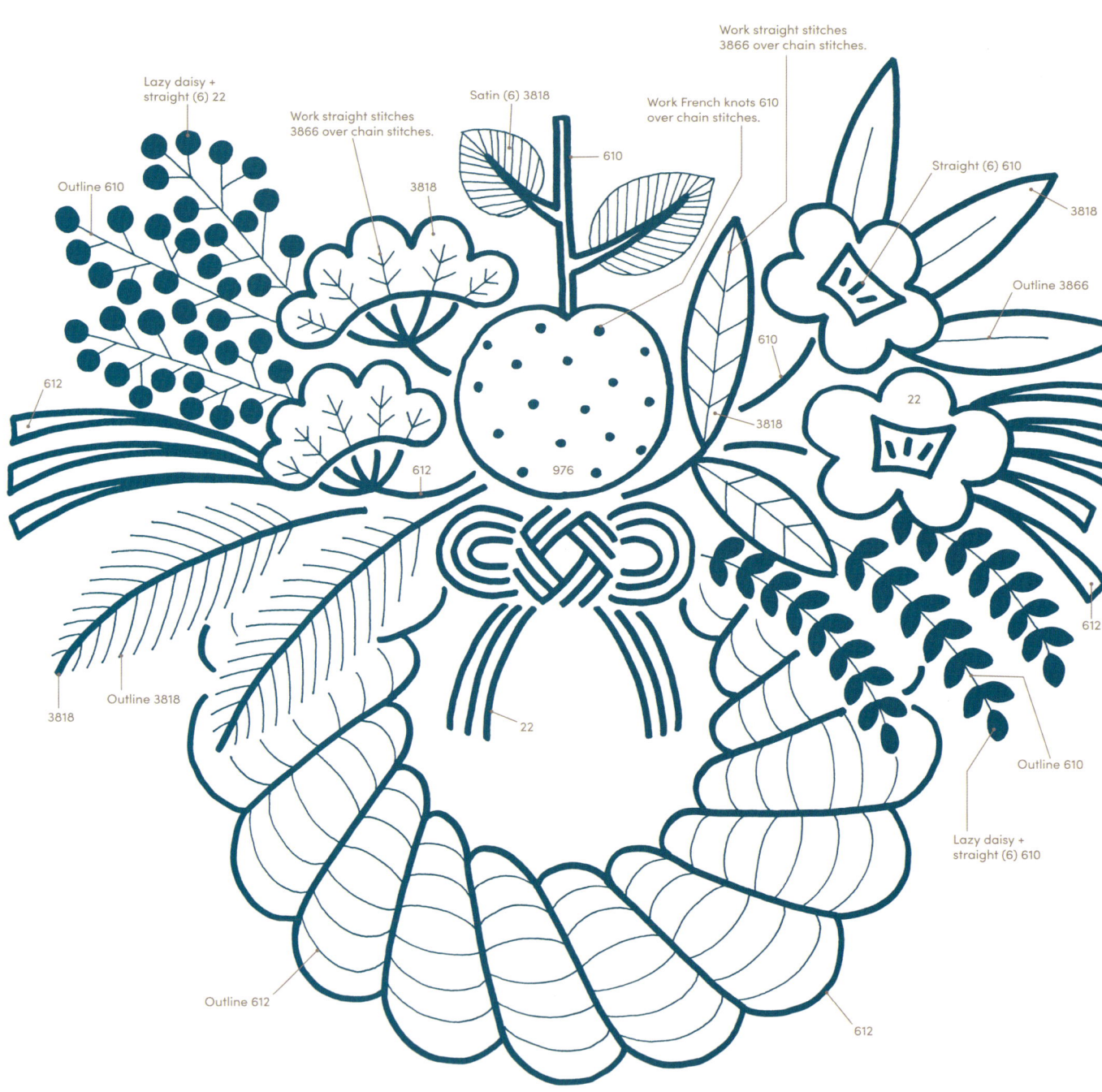

Lazy daisy +
straight (6) 22

Work straight stitches
3866 over chain stitches.

Satin (6) 3818

Work French knots 610
over chain stitches.

Work straight stitches
3866 over chain stitches.

Outline 610

3818

610

Straight (6) 610

3818

Outline 3866

612

610

3818

22

3818

976

612

22

612

3818

Outline 3818

Outline 610

Lazy daisy +
straight (6) 610

Outline 612

612

# Adonis Ramosa | page 8

*DMC No. 25 embroidery floss: 07, 08, 18, 520, 733, 3022, 3865
*Work chain stitch (2 strands), unless noted otherwise.
*Use 2 strands, unless noted otherwise.
*The number in parentheses is the number of strands, followed
  by the color code or name for the DMC No. 25 embroidery floss.

# Snowball Fight | page 9

*DMC No. 25 embroidery floss: 535, 611, 648, 930, 950, 3051, 3752, 3865
*Work chain stitch (2 strands) for lightly shaded areas.
*For faces, work satin stitch (4 strands) 950; and for hands, work French knots (6 strands) 3865.
*For dots [·] that are braids, work French knots (4 strands) in the same color as hair; and for dots [·] that are pom-poms, work French knots (4 strands) 3865 in the same color as hats.
*For all other stitches, work satin stitch (4 strands), unless noted otherwise.
*The number in parentheses is the number of strands, followed by the color code or name for the DMC No. 25 embroidery floss.

# Birds Singing in Spring | page 11

*DMC No. 25 embroidery floss: ecru, 310, 471, 936, 950, 3328, 3346, 3778, 3865
*Use 4 strands, unless noted otherwise.
*The number in parentheses is the number of strands, followed by the color code or name for the DMC No. 25 embroidery floss.

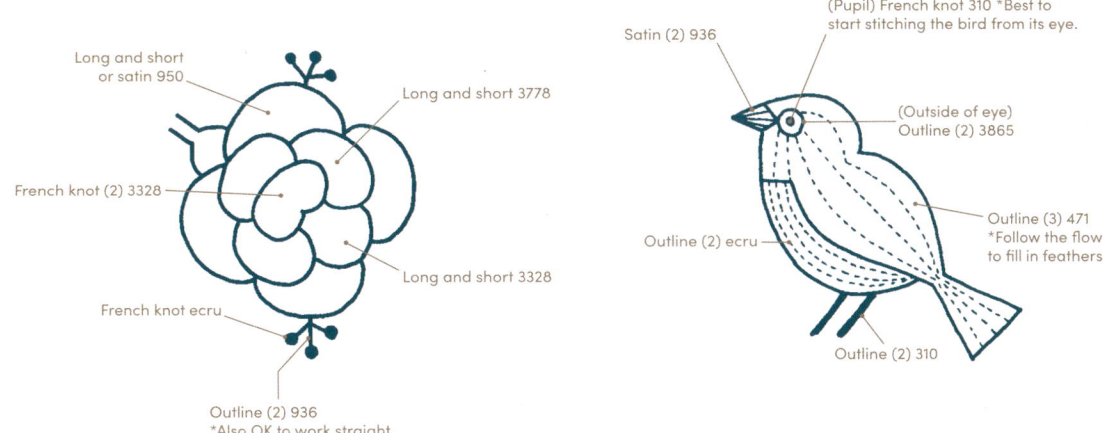

Long and short or satin 950

Long and short 3778

French knot (2) 3328

Long and short 3328

French knot ecru

Outline (2) 936
*Also OK to work straight.

Satin (2) 936

(Pupil) French knot 310 *Best to start stitching the bird from its eye.

(Outside of eye) Outline (2) 3865

Outline (3) 471 *Follow the flow to fill in feathers.

Outline (2) ecru

Outline (2) 310

French knot (6) 3328

Lazy daisy + straight 950

Lazy daisy + straight (6) 3346

Lazy daisy + straight (6) 936

Chain (2) 936

French knot 3778

Straight 3328

Outline (2) 3346

Long and short ecru

Chain (2) 936

Outline 3346

Satin 3346

Long and short 3328

Lazy daisy + straight 3346

Chain (2) 3346

French knot ecru

Outline (2) 936
*Work straight stitches for short lines.

Chain (2) 936

# Bouquet of Tulips | page 12

*DMC No. 25 embroidery floss: 150, 501, 502, 950, 3687
*Work chain stitch (2 strands), unless noted otherwise.
*The number in parentheses is the number of strands, followed by the color code or name for the DMC No. 25 embroidery floss.

# Violet Garden | page 16

*DMC No. 25 embroidery floss: 29, 500, 502, 561, 733, 3042, 3750, 3865
*The number in parentheses is the number of strands, followed by the color code or name for the DMC No. 25 embroidery floss.

Outline (3) 502

Long and short (4) 29

Straight (1) 3865

Long and short (4) 3750

Long and short (4) 3042

Work outline stitches (2) 500 over chain stitches.

Chain (2) 561

3687

150

950

501

150

Outline (2) 502

Work French knot (6) 3687 for the center of the bow.

Chain (2) 561

Work French knots (6) 733 over finished stitches.

Work straight stitches (4) 3865 over long and short stitches.

# Baking Sweets | page 13

*DMC No. 25 embroidery floss: 310, 645, 648, 739, 801, 833, 938, 986, 3350, 3371, 3865
*Work chain stitch (2 strands) for lightly shaded areas.
*For all other stitches, work satin stitch (4 strands), unless noted otherwise.
*The number in parentheses is the number of strands, followed by the color code or name for the DMC No. 25 embroidery floss.

938

French knot (2) 938

Outline (2) 645

739

645

801

3371

3865

833

645

648

648

648

648

739

645

3865

Work straight stitches (4) 3350 over chain stitches.

739

Work straight stitches (4) in 3350, 3865 & 986 for sprinkles.

648

801

Work backstitches (2) 3350 over chain stitches.

938

801

Lazy daisy + straight (4) 938

Work straight stitches (2) 645 over chain stitches.

Outline (2) 739

833

833

739

833

833

648

645

801

938

FLOUR

Work backstitches (2) 310 over chain stitches.

Work straight stitches (4) 833 over chain stitches.

645

Outline (2) 3371

938

801

645

801

Straight (2) 310

310

SUGAR

3865

French knot (2) 739

Lazy daisy + straight (3) 986

Work straight stitches (2) 648 over chain stitches.

648

Outline (2) 310

3865

645

3350

938

Work straight stitches (4) 739 over satin stitches.

645

310

645

Outline (2) 310

3371

801

801

3371

3865

986

Work straight stitches (2) 648 over chain stitches.

801

310

648

Outline (4) 3350

645

648

3865

Work French knots (4) 833 over chain stitches.

Work straight stitches (4) 3865 over satin stitches.

3865

Outline (4) 648

310

75

# Hinamatsuri—Girls' Day | page 15

*DMC No. 25 embroidery floss: 22, 168, 543, 839, 936, 3371, 3687, 3866, E677
*Work outline stitch (1 strand) 3371 for thick lines.
*Work chain stitch (2 strands), unless noted otherwise.
*Use 2 strands, unless noted otherwise.
*The number in parentheses is the number of strands, followed by the color
 code or name for the DMC No. 25 embroidery floss.

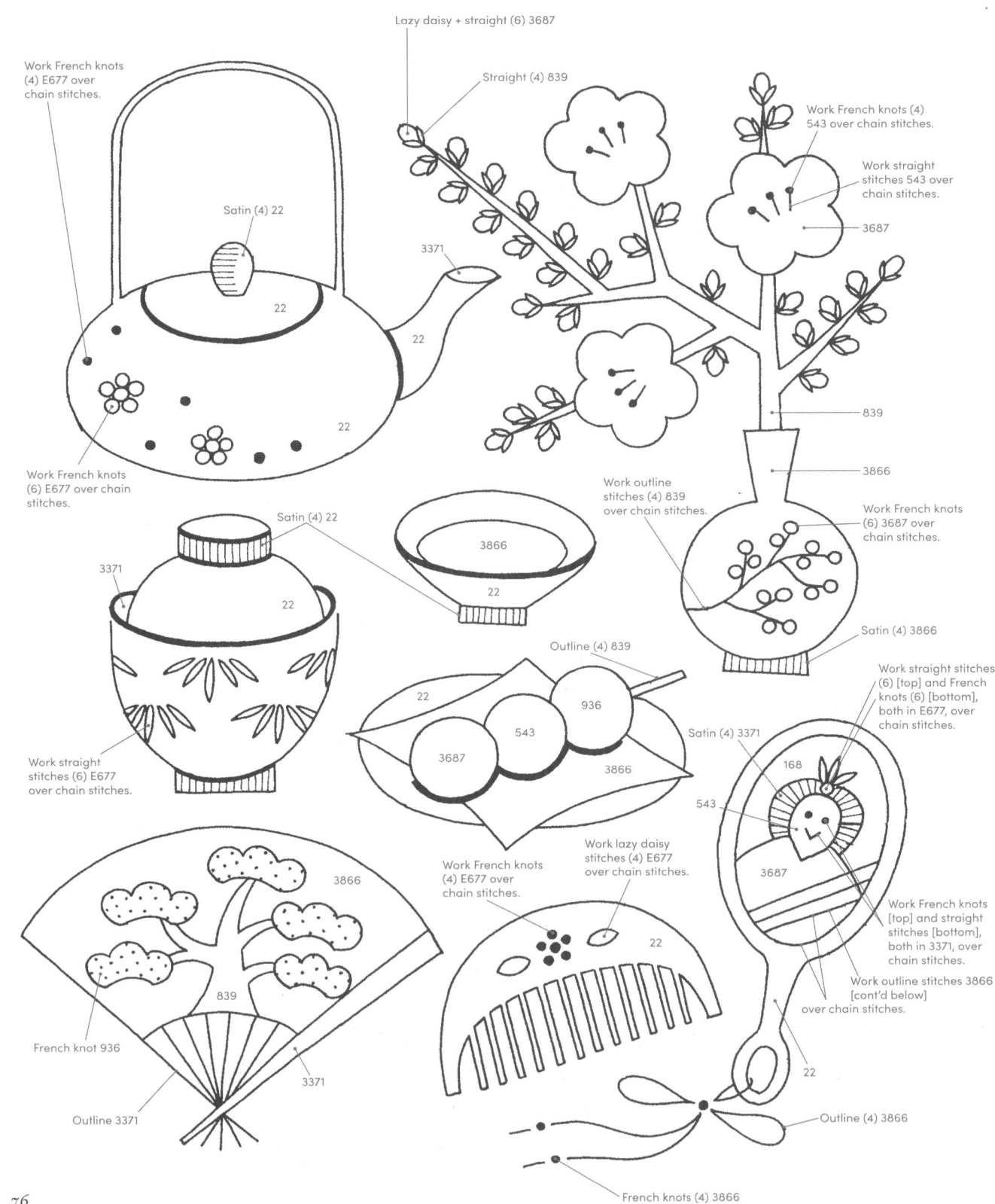

Lazy daisy + straight (6) 3687

Straight (4) 839

Work French knots
(4) E677 over
chain stitches.

Work French knots (4)
543 over chain stitches.

Work straight
stitches 543 over
chain stitches.

3687

Satin (4) 22

3371

22

22

839

22

3866

Work French knots
(6) E677 over chain
stitches.

Satin (4) 22

3371

22

Work outline
stitches (4) 839
over chain stitches.

3866

22

Work French knots
(6) 3687 over
chain stitches.

Work straight
stitches (6) E677
over chain stitches.

Outline (4) 839

936

3687   543

3866

Satin (4) 3866

Work straight stitches
(6) [top] and French
knots (6) [bottom],
both in E677, over
chain stitches.

Satin (4) 3371

168

543

3687

Work French knots
[top] and straight
stitches [bottom],
both in 3371, over
chain stitches.

3866

Work French knots
(4) E677 over
chain stitches.

Work lazy daisy
stitches (4) E677
over chain stitches.

22

French knot 936

839

Outline 3371

3371

22

Work outline stitches 3866
[cont'd below]
over chain stitches.

Outline (4) 3866

French knots (4) 3866

76

# Easter Eggs | page 19

*DMC No. 25 embroidery floss: 336, 3865
*Work outline stitch (1 strand) for thin lines, unless noted otherwise.
*Use 336, unless noted otherwise.
*The number in parentheses is the number of strands, followed by the color code or name for the DMC No. 25 embroidery floss.
*For appliqués, attach double-sided fusible interfacing to the reverse side of the cut-out egg shapes, then sew with slip stitches all the way around. I recommend using batiste or sheeting for the cotton fabric.

Straight (1)

French knot (2)

For eye, work French knot (2) 3865 over chain stitches.

Lazy daisy + straight (2)

Chain (2)

Chain (2)

Outline (2)

Straight (2)

Lazy daisy + straight (2)

Lazy daisy + straight (2)

French knot (2)

Lazy daisy + straight (2)

Chain (2)

French knot (2)

Lazy daisy + straight (2)

# Gardening | page 20

*DMC No. 25 embroidery floss: ecru, 03, 04, 33, 310, 834, 986,
  3031, 3364, 3782, 3790, 3836
*Work chain stitch (2 strands), unless noted otherwise.
*Use 2 strands, unless noted otherwise.
*The number in parentheses is the number of strands, followed by
  the color code or name for the DMC No. 25 embroidery floss.

Straight (6) 33

French knot 3836

Lazy daisy +
straight 986

Satin (4) 3364

Satin (4)
3364

French knot 3836

Outline (1) 986

French knot (6) 33

Work straight stitches (1)
986 over chain stitches.

Work French knot in
ecru over chain stitches.

Satin (6) 3031

Outline (1) 3364

3782

French knot
(4) 3364

986

Work straight
stitches 3031
over chain
stitches.

310

3790

Satin (6) 3031

Outline 3031

3782

03

Satin (6) 3364

Satin (6)
986

Outline (4)
3364

Lazy daisy +
straight 986

Outline (1) 3364

Outline (1)
3031

Satin (6) 04

04

04

Outline (1)
3031

Satin (6) 3790

Straight
310

04

French knot (4) ecru

Lazy daisy +
straight 986

03

Outline (1) 986

Lazy daisy +
straight (4) 3364

3836

Work straight
stitches 310
over chain
stitches.

Satin (6) 33

3790

986

Outline
(1) 3790

Satin (4) 3364

SEEDS

Outline (4) 3031

3782

986

310

986

Satin (6) 986

Outline (1) 3364

Outline (1) 3364

Straight
(4) 986

3790

Straight
(1) 310

03

834

Work straight
stitches (6) 310 over
chain stitches.

Satin (6) 310

04

78

# Stationery | page 21

*DMC No. 25 embroidery floss: 310, 311, 535, 611, 648, 739, 3362
*Work French knots (6 strands) for dots [·] over stitches for base color.
*Work satin stitch (4 strands) for striped areas.
*For all other stitches, work chain stitch (2 strands), unless noted otherwise.
*Use 2 strands, unless noted otherwise.
*The number in parentheses is the number of strands, followed by the color
  code or name for the DMC No. 25 embroidery floss.

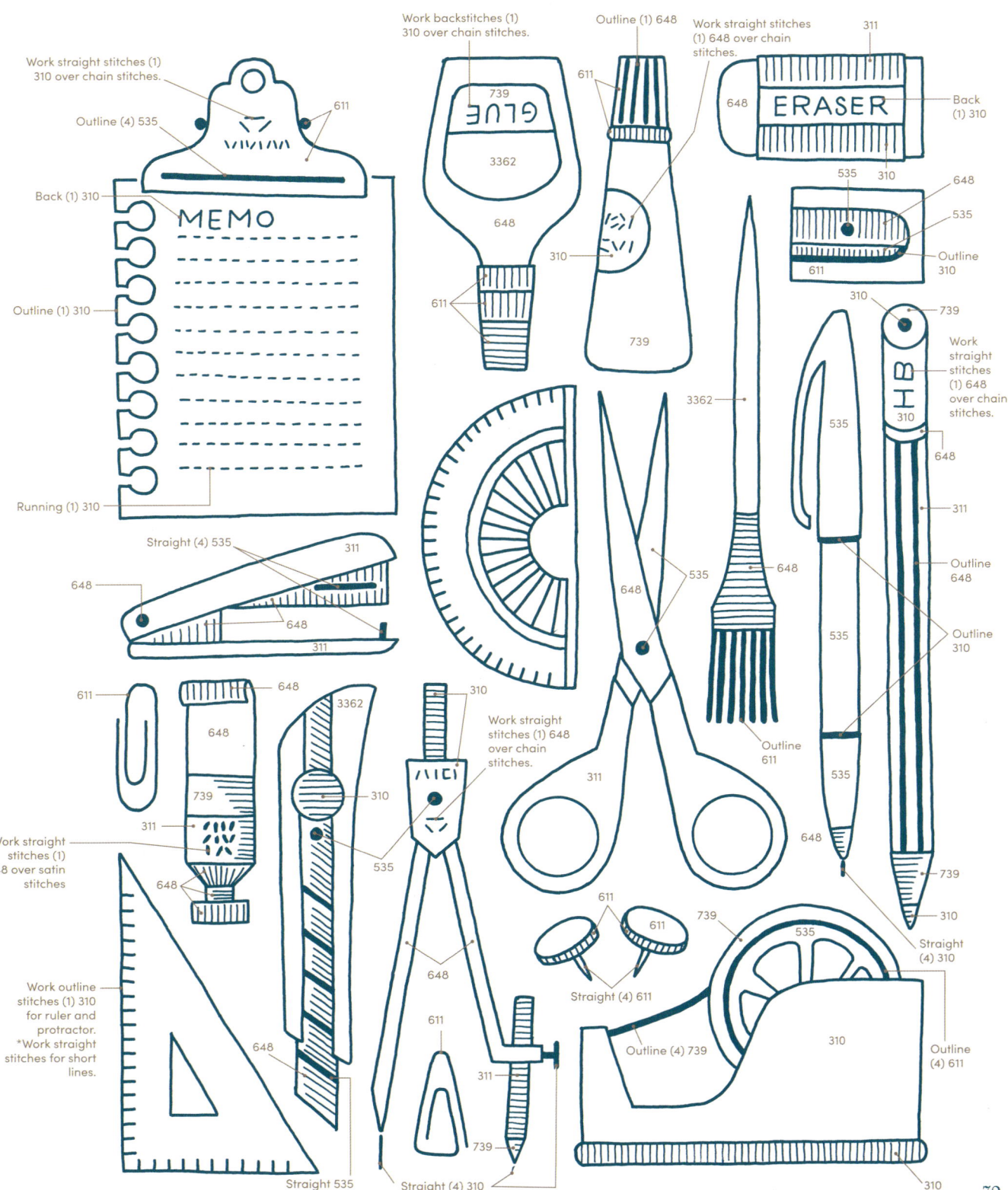

# Travel | page 23

*DMC No. 25 embroidery floss: 03, 22, 310, 535, 561, 612, 833, 931, 3021, 3865
*Work chain stitch (2 strands), unless noted otherwise.
*Use 2 strands, unless noted otherwise.
*The number in parentheses is the number of strands, followed by the color code or name for the DMC No. 25 embroidery floss.

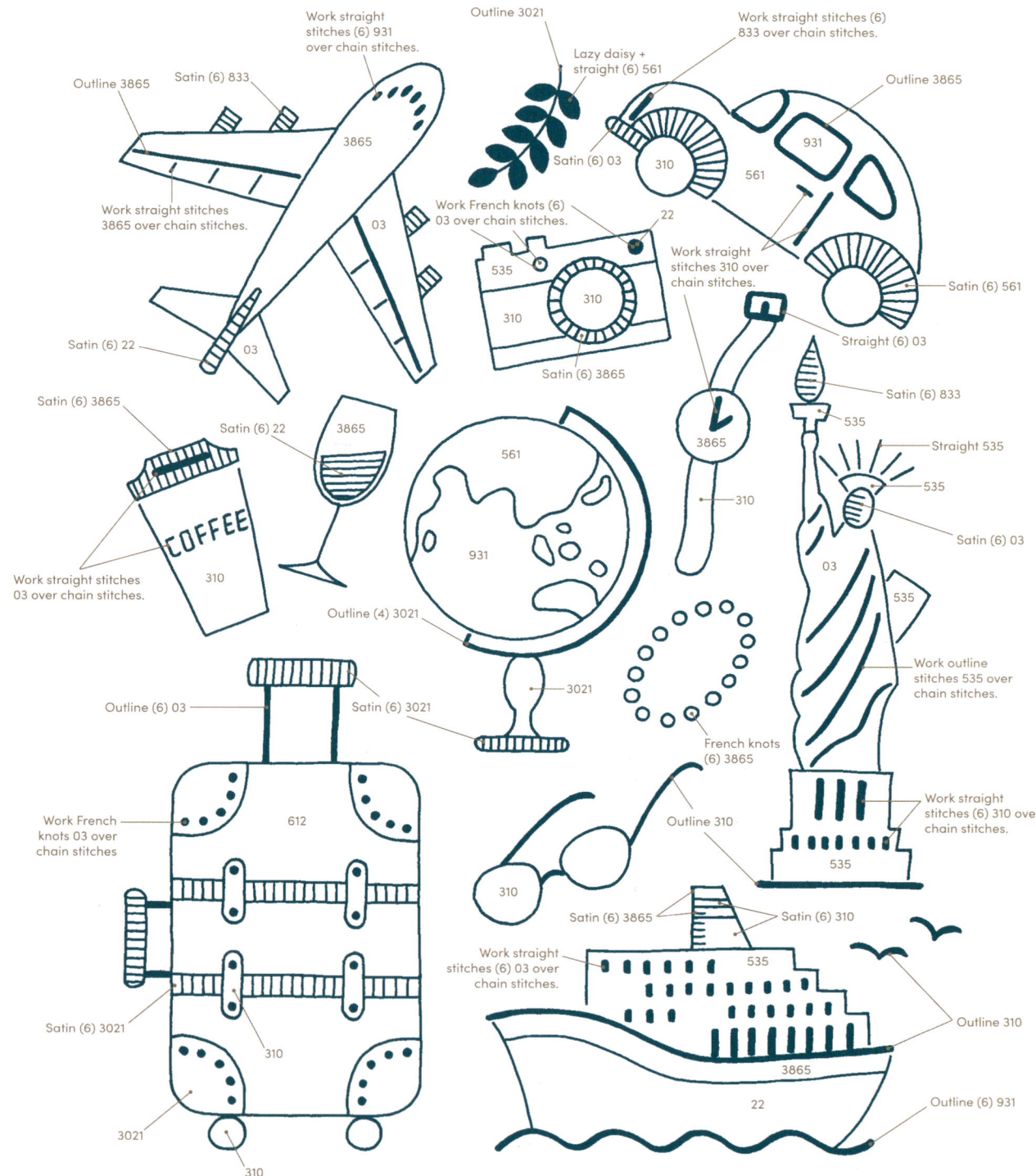

Work straight stitches (6) 931 over chain stitches.

Outline 3865

Lazy daisy + straight (6) 561

Work straight stitches (6) 833 over chain stitches.

Outline 3865

Outline 3865

Satin (6) 833

3865

931

561

Work straight stitches 3865 over chain stitches.

3865

03

Satin (6) 03

Work French knots (6) 03 over chain stitches.

22

310

Work straight stitches 310 over chain stitches.

Satin (6) 561

Satin (6) 22

03

535

310

310

Satin (6) 3865

Straight (6) 03

Satin (6) 3865

Satin (6) 22

3865

561

3865

310

Satin (6) 833

535

Straight 535

535

Satin (6) 03

COFFEE

310

Work straight stitches 03 over chain stitches.

931

Outline (4) 3021

03

535

Work outline stitches 535 over chain stitches.

Outline (6) 03

Satin (6) 3021

3021

French knots (6) 3865

Outline 310

Work French knots 03 over chain stitches

612

Work straight stitches (6) 310 over chain stitches.

535

310

Satin (6) 3021

310

Satin (6) 3865

Satin (6) 310

Work straight stitches (6) 03 over chain stitches.

535

Outline 310

3021

310

3865

22

Outline (6) 931

80

# Spring Wreath | page 24

*DMC No. 25 embroidery floss: 154, 320, 505, 561, 632, 733, 739, 3042, 3813, 3815, 3865
*Work outline stitch (3 strands) 632 for thick lines.
*Work chain stitch (3 strands) 561 for lightly shaded areas.
*For all other stitches, work outline stitch (2 strands) 320, unless noted otherwise.
*The number in parentheses is the number of strands, followed by the color code or
  name for the DMC No. 25 embroidery floss.

**Enlarge by 110 percent.**

Outline (2) 3815

Satin (4) 561

French knot (2) 3813

Outline (4) 320

French knot (4) 733

French knot (4) 733

Straight (2) 320

French knot (6) 739

Outline (1) 320

French knot (6) 3042

French knot (6) 154

Satin (4) 561

Lazy daisy +
straight (6) 3865

Lazy daisy +
straight (4) 505

Outline (2) 505

(Flower center)
French knot (6) 739

# Koinobori (Carp Streamer) Tapestry | page 25

*DMC No. 25 embroidery floss: 07, 22, 310, 327, 505, 794, 833, 3865
*Work outline stitch for thick lines.
*Work French knots for dots [·] and circles [°].
*Work chain stitch (2 strands) for lightly shaded areas.
*The number in parentheses is the number of strands, followed by
  the color code or name for the DMC No. 25 embroidery floss.

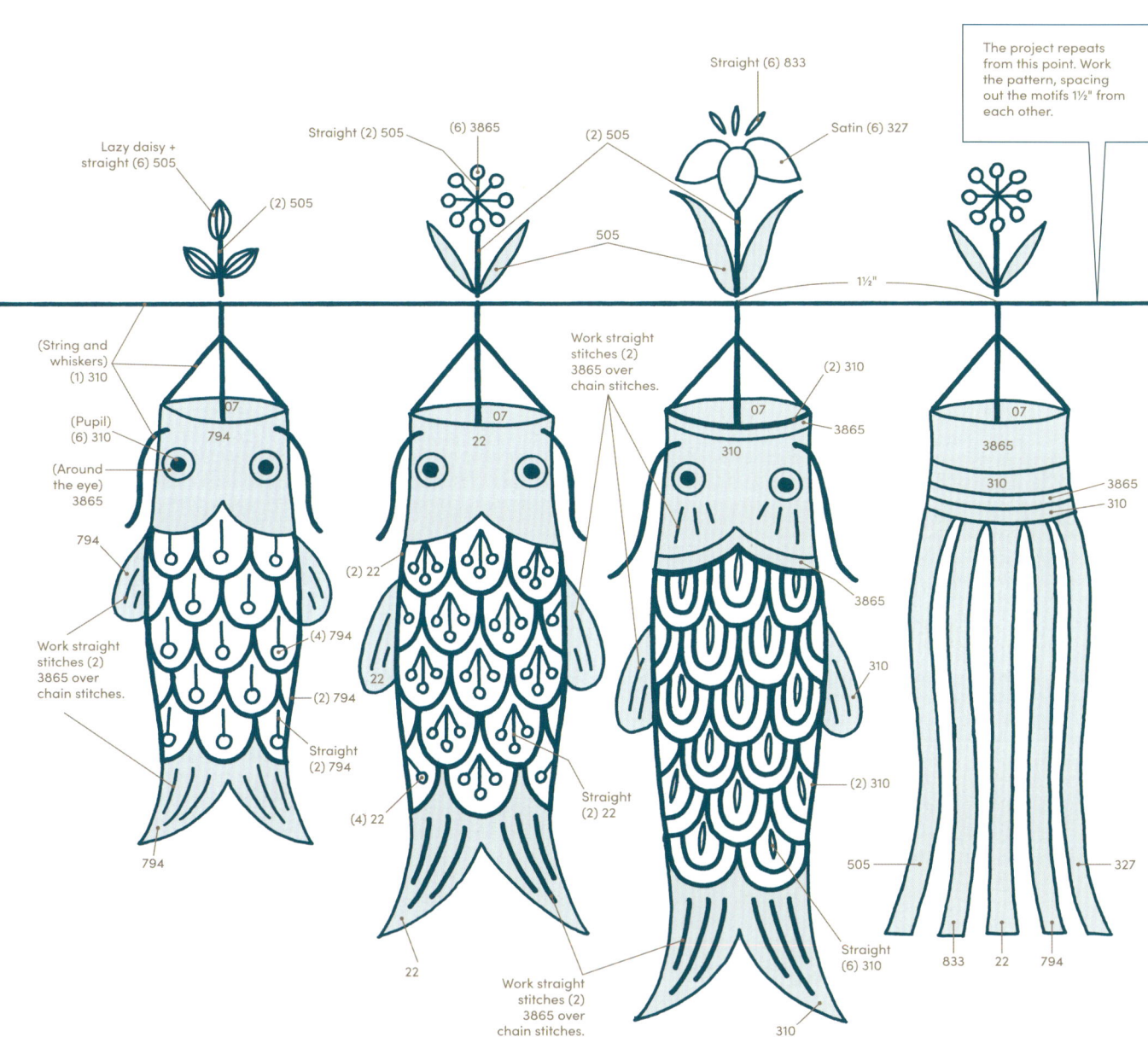

# Passion Flower Wreath | page 27

*DMC No. 25 embroidery floss: 01, 32, 154, 310, 319, 505, 522, 3348
*Work chain stitch (2 strands), unless noted otherwise.
*Use 2 strands, unless noted otherwise.
*The number in parentheses is the number of strands, followed by
  the color code or name for the DMC No. 25 embroidery floss.

Outline (4) 319

Work outline
stitches 32 over
chain stitches.

01

Straight (1) 310

French knot (6) 310

01

Straight (6) 3348

Satin (6) 310

Work straight
stitches 32 over
long and short
stitches.

Long and
short (6) 01

French knot (6)
Straight (6),
both 154

Straight (6)
French knot (6),
both 3348

Satin (6) 522

Outline (3) 522

505

# Wedding | page 28

*DMC No. 25 embroidery floss: 470, 645, 832, 910 (2 skeins), 931, 950, 3865
*Work outline stitch (2 strands) 470 for thick lines.
*Work French knots (4 strands) for circles [°].
*Work satin stitch for lightly shaded areas.
*The number in parentheses is the number of strands, followed by the color
 code or name for the DMC No. 25 embroidery floss.

Lazy daisy + straight (3) 910

Lazy daisy + straight (6) 3865

Work straight stitches (4) 910 over lazy daisy + straight stitches.

(6) 910

Outline (2) 3865

(2) 832

(4) 3865

Straight (4) 910

(4) 931

(4) 910

(4) 832

(4) 950

832

3865

(4) 3865

(4) 3865

(6) 910

Straight (4) 3865

(4) 950

(4) 645

Chain (2) 3865

Outline (2) 910

3865

(4) 470

(6) 910

French knot (2) 832

Long and short (6) 3865

(4) 910

84

# Teatime | page 29

*DMC No. 25 embroidery floss: 04, 224, 505, 739, 918, 989, 3865
*Work satin stitch (4 strands) for striped areas.
*For all other stitches, work outline stitch, unless noted otherwise.

*The number in parentheses is the number of strands, followed by the color code or name for the DMC No. 25 embroidery floss.
*Use the dotted lines as approximate guides for where to connect the repeating pattern.

(a)

Continue from (a)

(2) 224

224

(2) 3865

(b)

(3) 918

Lazy daisy + straight (4) 505

739

918

Chain (2) 04

Center point of panel

Lazy daisy + straight (4) 3865

3865

Lazy daisy + straight (6) 739

Chain (2) 04

Chain (2) 3865

French knot (4) 224

3865

Chain (2) 918

Chain (2) 04

(2) 989

Satin (6) 505

Continue from (b)

Chain (2) 3865

# Cocktails | page 31

*DMC No. 25 embroidery floss: 18, 310, 645, 677, 721, 758, 791, 900, 932, 988,
  991, 993, 3866
*Work outline stitch for thick lines.
*Work satin stitch (4 strands) for striped areas.
*For circles [°], work French knots (2 strands) over chain stitches.
*For all glasses, work chain stitch (2 strands) 3866.
*For all other stitches, work chain stitch (2 strands), unless noted otherwise.
*The number in parentheses is the number of strands, followed by the color
  code or name for the DMC No. 25 embroidery floss.

TIP

When filling in
round areas with
satin stitches, work
outline stitches
(2) underneath
to help create
uniform shapes.

# Cactus Pattern | page 33

*DMC No. 25 embroidery floss: 01, 03, 319, 368, 505, 535, 3021, 3022, 3790, 3865
*Work chain stitch (2 strands), unless noted otherwise.
*The number in parentheses is the number of strands, followed by the color code or name for the DMC No. 25 embroidery floss.

Lazy daisy + straight (4) 368

Work straight stitches (1) 3865 over chain stitches.

Satin (6) 319

Straight (2) 319

319

Work French knots (2) 3022 over chain stitches.

Work French knots (2) 3865 over chain stitches.

Work French knots (2) 319 over chain stitches.

Satin (6) 3022

Straight (2) 3865

Outline (2) 3022

French knot (4) 535

French knot (4) 03

French knot (4) 03

French knot (4) 01

Satin (6) 319

505

368

505

319

505

03

01

3021

03

3021

3790

3021

Work straight stitches (2) 3865 over chain stitches.

Satin (6) 01

Work straight stitches (4) 535 over chain stitches.

Work straight stitches (2) 3865 over chain stitches.

# Blue Flowers in Summer | page 34

*DMC No. 25 embroidery floss: ecru, 336, 368, 505, 561, 793, 798, 800
*The number in parentheses is the number of strands, followed by the color code or name for the DMC No. 25 embroidery floss.

Outline (4) 505

Lazy daisy + straight (4) 561

(Flower center and bud) French knot (6) 798

Lazy daisy + straight (3) ecru

Satin (4) 798

Lazy daisy + straight (4) 800

Outline (2) 336

(Flower center) French knot (4) 368

French knot (4) ecru

Work straight stitches (3) ecru over long and short stitches.

Long and short (4) 798

Long and short (4) 793

Outline (4) 368

Lazy daisy + straight (4) 505

Satin (4) 505

Outline (2) 368

French knot (4) 793

Satin (4) 561

# Coral Forest | page 37

*DMC No. 25 embroidery floss: ecru, 22, 165, 310, 367, 471, 543, 758, 3042, 3768, 3778
*Work French knots for dots [·] and circles [°].
*Work chain stitch (2 strands), unless noted otherwise.

*Use 2 strands, unless noted otherwise.
*The number in parentheses is the number of strands, followed by the color code or name for the DMC No. 25 embroidery floss.

Work straight stitches (4) ecru over chain stitches.

Outline (1) 3768

165

ecru

165

(6) ecru

Work straight stitches in ecru over chain stitches.

758

22

Work (4) 22 over chain stitches.

367

(4) 3778

Work 310 over chain stitches.

543

ecru

Work 758 over chain stitches.

471

Work outline stitches in ecru over chain stitches.

Straight (4) 3768

758

310

ecru

3768

3778

Satin (4) 3768

Outline 3042

Straight (4) ecru

3042

Work 471 over chain stitches.

Work 367 over chain stitches.

Work straight stitches 22 over chain stitches.

367

367

Outline 367

758

543

165

Work straight stitches in ecru over chain stitches.

Outline (4) 3768

Straight ecru

Work ecru over chain stitches.

88

# Summer Foods | page 38

*DMC No. 25 embroidery floss: 17, 310, 320, 349, 648, 699, 800, 825, 3862
*Work outline stitch for thick lines.
*Work satin stitch for striped areas.
*Work French knots (2 strands) for dots [·].
*For all other stitches, work chain stitch (2 strands), unless noted otherwise.
*The number in parentheses is the number of strands, followed by the color
  code or name for the DMC No. 25 embroidery floss.

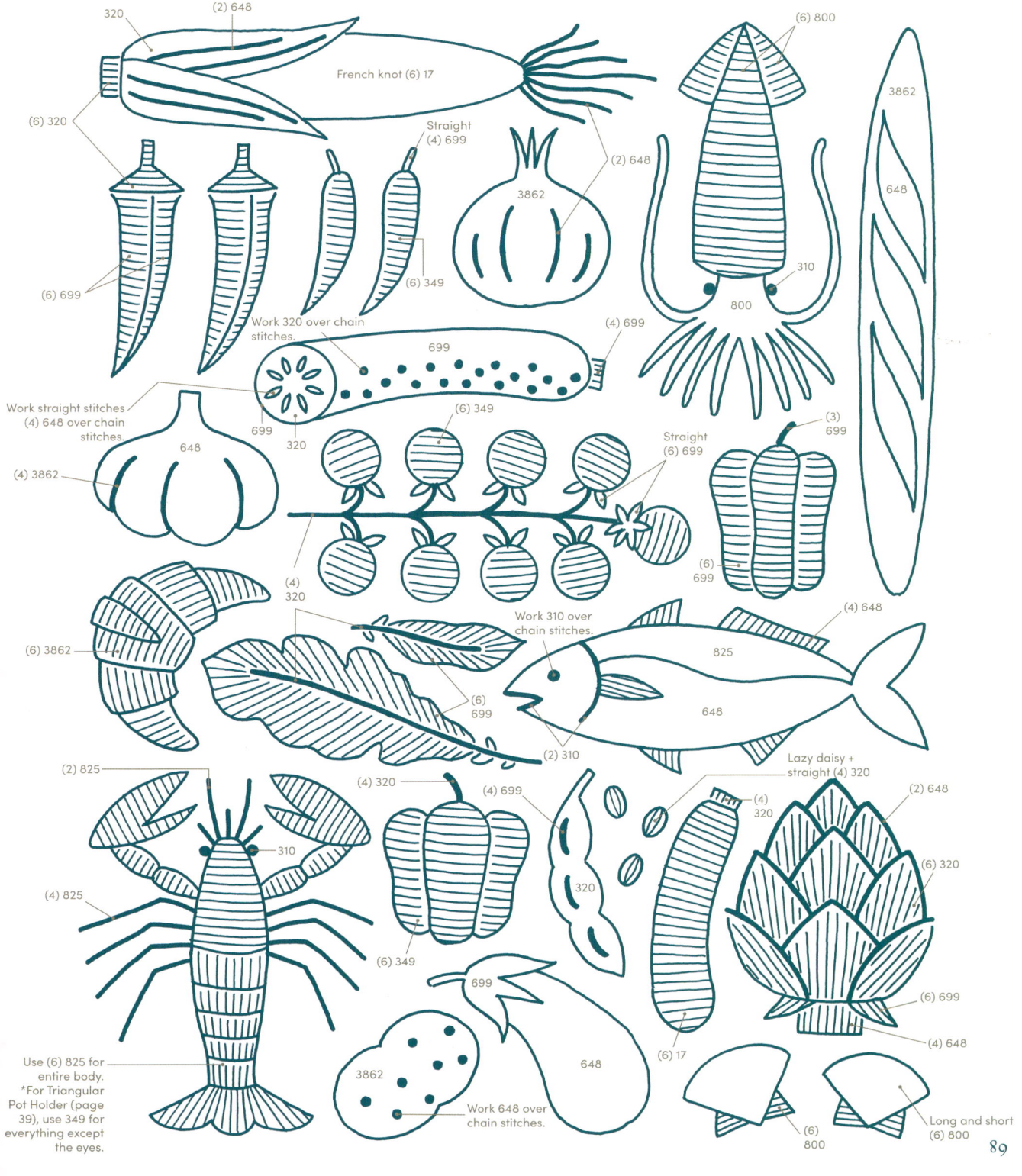

320

(2) 648

French knot (6) 17

(6) 800

3862

648

(6) 320

Straight
(4) 699

(2) 648

310

800

(6) 699

(6) 349

3862

Work 320 over chain
stitches.

699

(4) 699

Work straight stitches
(4) 648 over chain
stitches.

699

320

648

(6) 349

Straight
(6) 699

(3)
699

(4) 3862

(4)
320

(6)
699

(6) 3862

Work 310 over
chain stitches.

(4) 648

825

648

(6)
699

(2) 310

Lazy daisy +
straight (4) 320

(2) 825

(4) 320

(4) 699

(4)
320

(2) 648

310

(6) 320

(4) 825

320

(6) 699

(6) 349

699

(6) 17

(4) 648

Use (6) 825 for
entire body.
*For Triangular
Pot Holder (page
39), use 349 for
everything except
the eyes.

3862

648

Work 648 over
chain stitches.

(6)
800

Long and short
(6) 800

89

# Seven Flowers of Autumn | page 41

*DMC No. 25 embroidery floss: 32, 520, 543, 833, 915, 935, 939, 3607
*Use 2 strands, unless noted otherwise.
*The number in parentheses is the number of strands, followed by
  the color code or name for the DMC No. 25 embroidery floss.

Outline 935

Outline 3607

Chain 520

Lazy daisy + straight 915

French knot (4) 543

Work straight stitches 939 over satin stitches.

Satin (6) 32

French knot (4) 543

Lazy daisy + straight (6) 520

Outline 935

French knot (6) 833

French knot (4) 543

Lazy daisy + straight 3607

Lazy daisy + straight (4) 915

Satin (6) 520

Outline 935

Outline 543

Chain 520

French knot (4) 3607

Outline 543

Chain 935

Chain 520

French knot 543

Outline 915

# Musical Instruments | page 42

*DMC No. 25 embroidery floss: ecru, 310, 610, 645, 801
*Work satin stitch (4 strands) for lightly shaded areas.
*For all other stitches, work chain stitch (2 strands), unless noted otherwise.
*The number in parentheses is the number of strands, followed by the color
 code or name for the DMC No. 25 embroidery floss.

801

610

610

Straight (2) 310

645

Work outline
stitches (1)
ecru over
chain stitches.

801

645

Work French knots
(2) ecru over
chain stitches.

Straight (2) 645

Outline (2) 645

Straight (4) 310

ecru

801

801

801

801

310

Outline (2) 610

Work French knots (2)
610 over satin stitches.

310

Straight (6) 645

610

French knot (6) 645

Outline
(2) ecru

610

310

ecru

Outline (4) 645

310

ecru

310

310

310

645

Straight (4) 310

ecru

645

610

French knot (4) 801

Straight
(2) 310

801

Outline (1) 310

Straight (2) 610

Outline (2) 310

310

645
*Work chain
stitches
underneath.

French knot (3) 645

Outline (4) 610

ecru

French knot (4) 310

310

645

310

610

Outline
(3) 645

Outline (1) 310

Work straight
stitches
(2) 310
over chain
stitches.

310

310

310

801

ecru

801

Work straight
stitches (1)
310 over all
stitches.

310

Work straight stitches (4) 610
over all stitches each time.

# Pumpkin Patch | page 45

*DMC No. 25 embroidery floss: 832, 919, 921, 935, 976, 3022, 3064
*For stems, work outline stitch (6 strands) 3022 for thick lines and outline stitch (3 strands) 3022 for thin lines.

*For all other stitches, work chain stitch (2 strands), unless noted otherwise.
*The number in parentheses is the number of strands, followed by the color code or name for the DMC No. 25 embroidery floss.

Lazy daisy +
straight (4) 935

Lazy daisy +
straight (6) 832

French knot
(3) 3022

935

Work straight
stitches (1) 3022
over chain stitches.

919

Lazy daisy +
straight (4) 3022

Outline (2) 919

921

3064

Outline
(2) 3064

919

976

# Book Cover with Fallen Leaves | page 51

*DMC No. 25 embroidery floss:
07, 300, 646, 829, 898, 918, 3031
*Use 2 strands, unless noted otherwise.
*The number in parentheses is the number of strands,
followed by the color code or name for the DMC No. 25
embroidery floss.

Outline 829

Outline 918

Long and short
(4) 829

Chain 918

Straight 3031

Satin (4) 3031

Satin (4) 07

Chain 300

Outline 300

Satin (4) 898

Outline 898

Straight 646

92

# Pear Pattern | page 46

*DMC No. 25 embroidery floss: ecru, 522 (2 skeins), 831 (3 skeins),
839 (2 skeins), 3362 (6 skeins)
*Work outline stitch, unless noted otherwise.

*The number in parentheses is the number of strands, followed
by the color code or name for the DMC No. 25 embroidery floss.
*Use the dotted lines as approximate guides for where to
connect the repeating pattern.

Continue from (a)

(4) 522

Satin (6) 3362

Lazy daisy +
straight (6) 522

Long and
short (6) ecru

Chain (3) 3362

Straight
(6) 3362

(3) 3362

Satin (6) 831

French knot (3) 831

Center point
of panel

Satin (6) 3362

Straight (3) 3362

(6)
839

(4) 522

Chain (3) 831

Chain (3) 839

Satin
(6) 831

Lazy daisy +
straight (4)
3362

Straight
(3) 522

French knot
(6) 831

Continue from (b)

# Autumn Wreath | page 49

*DMC No. 25 embroidery floss: 07, 08, 29, 224, 300, 520, 3371, 3722, 3782, 3866
*Work outline stitch (6 strands) 3371 for thick lines.
*For all other stitches, work outline stitch, unless noted otherwise.
*The number in parentheses is the number of strands, followed by the color
  code or name for the DMC No. 25 embroidery floss.

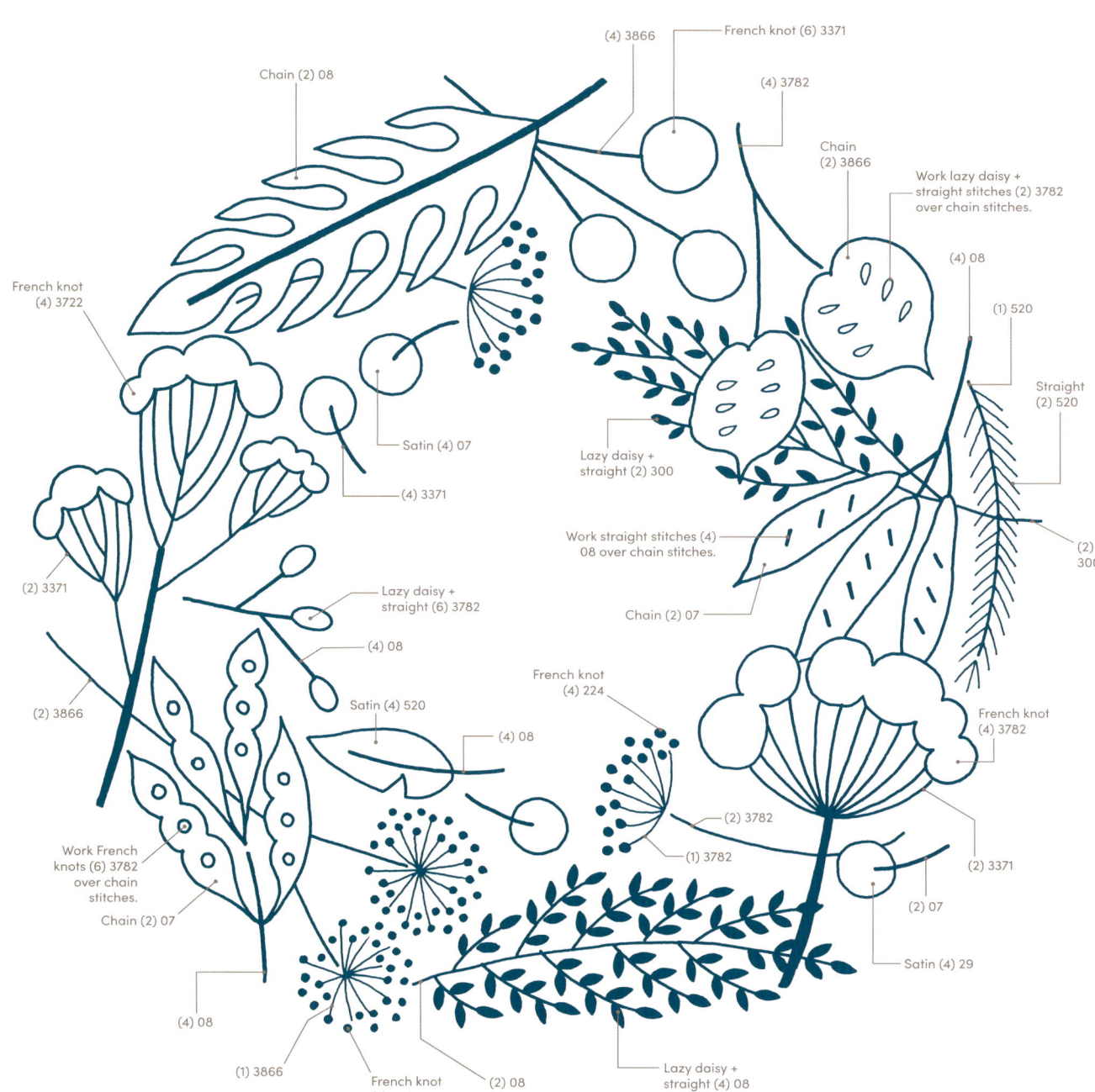

Chain (2) 08

(4) 3866

French knot (6) 3371

(4) 3782

Chain (2) 3866

Work lazy daisy + straight stitches (2) 3782 over chain stitches.

(4) 08

(1) 520

French knot (4) 3722

Straight (2) 520

Satin (4) 07

(4) 3371

Lazy daisy + straight (2) 300

Work straight stitches (4) 08 over chain stitches.

(2) 300

(2) 3371

Lazy daisy + straight (6) 3782

(4) 08

Chain (2) 07

French knot (4) 3782

(2) 3866

Satin (4) 520

French knot (4) 224

(4) 08

French knot (4) 3782

(2) 3782

(2) 3371

Work French knots (6) 3782 over chain stitches.

(1) 3782

(2) 07

Chain (2) 07

Satin (4) 29

(4) 08

(1) 3866

French knot (2) 3866

(2) 08

Lazy daisy + straight (4) 08

# Cozy Time at Home | page 50

*DMC No. 25 embroidery floss: 03, 07, 310, 407, 520, 839, 3721, 3750, 3866
*Work French knots for dots [·].
*Work outline stitch for thick lines.
*Work satin stitch (4 strands) for lightly shaded areas.
*For all other stitches, work chain stitch (2 strands), unless noted otherwise.

*The number in parentheses is the number of strands, followed by the color code or name for the DMC No. 25 embroidery floss.
*For printed text and images on book pages, work over chain stitches.
*For design on cushion, work over chain stitches.
*For stems and leaves of hanging plant, work over chain and outline stitches.

# Handknit Mittens | page 53

*DMC No. 25 embroidery floss: 07, 535, 3021, 3777, 3865
*Work French knots for dots [·].
*For all other stitches, work chain stitch (2 strands), unless noted otherwise.
*The number in parentheses is the number of strands, followed by the color
  code or name for the DMC No. 25 embroidery floss.

535

Work (2) 3865 over chain stitches.

3865

Outline (2) 535

3777

3865

Work straight stitches (4) 3777 over chain stitches.

3865

Work straight stitches (4) 3865 over chain stitches.

3865

Work (2) 3865 over chain stitches.

Work (2) 3777 over chain stitches.

3777

Work straight stitches (4) 3777 over chain stitches.

3865

Outline (2) 3777

Outline (2) 3021

07

Work straight stitches (4) 535 over chain stitches.

Work (2) 3777 over chain stitches.

3777

3865

Straight (6) 3777

(4) 535

535

Work (2) 3865 over chain stitches.

(2) 07

Work straight stitches (2) 3865 over chain stitches.

Straight (2) 3021

3021

3777

Outline (2) 535
*Work straight stitches for short lines.

(2) 535

Work straight stitches (4) 3865 over chain stitches.

3777

Work (2) 3865 over chain stitches.

3021

3865

Work (2) 3021 over chain stitches.

3021

3865

Work as for mitten on upper right.

Work (2) 07 over chain stitches.

Straight (4) 535

Straight (6) 3865

Straight (6) 3777

3777

3777

3021

Outline (2) 3865

07

07

3021

Straight (6) 3021

(4) 07

# Ribbon Brooch | page 54

*DMC No. 25 embroidery floss: (Christmas rose; same color scheme for A and C) 319, 407, 3022, 3866; (Stardust) ecru (D) 733 (B)
*The number in parentheses is the number of strands, followed by the color code or name for the DMC No. 25 embroidery floss.

[Christmas rose A, C]

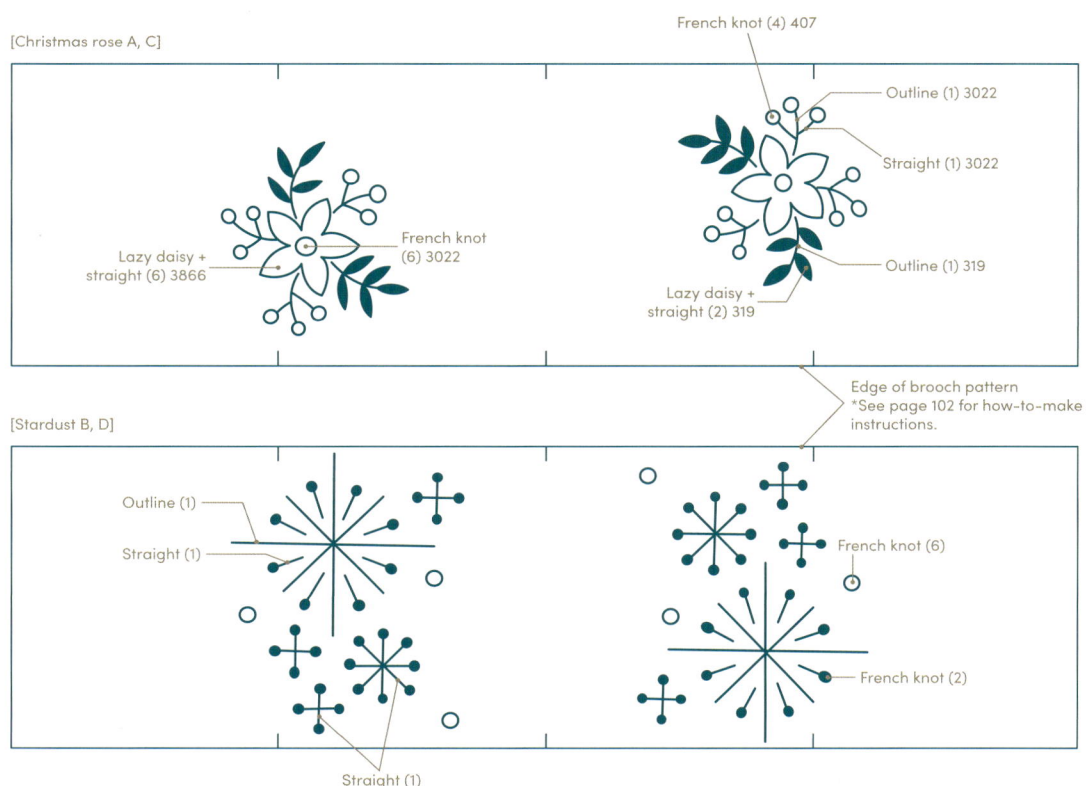

French knot (4) 407

Outline (1) 3022

Straight (1) 3022

Outline (1) 319

Lazy daisy + straight (2) 319

French knot (6) 3022

Lazy daisy + straight (6) 3866

Edge of brooch pattern
*See page 102 for how-to-make instructions.

[Stardust B, D]

Outline (1)

Straight (1)

French knot (6)

French knot (2)

Straight (1)

# Nutcracker Doll | page 55

*DMC No. 25 embroidery floss: 310, 414, 824, 950, 3045, 3808, 3859, 3865
*Work French knots (4 strands) for dots [·].
*Work straight stitch for thick lines.
*Work satin stitch (4 strands) for lightly shaded areas.
*For all other stitches, work chain stitch (2 strands), unless noted otherwise.
*The number in parentheses is the number of strands, followed by the color code or name for the DMC No. 25 embroidery floss.

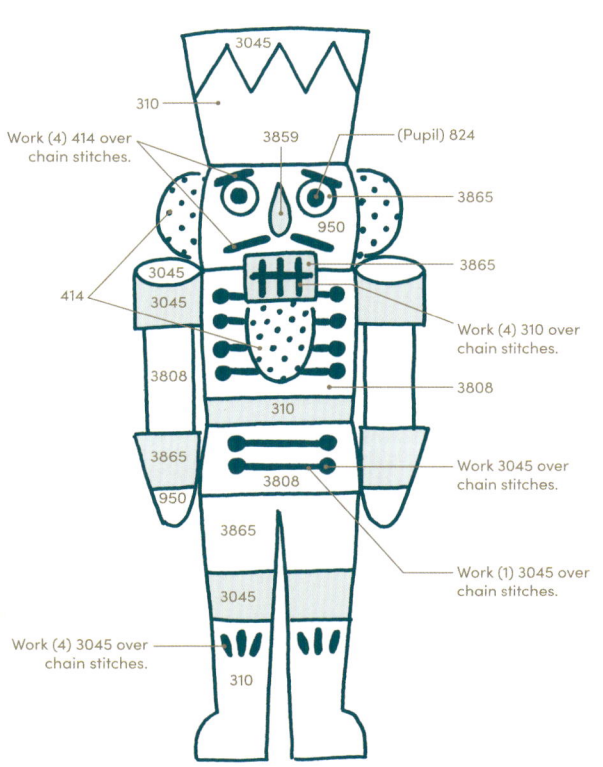

3045

310

Work (4) 414 over chain stitches.

3859

(Pupil) 824

3865

950

3045

3045

3865

414

Work (4) 310 over chain stitches.

3808

3808

310

3865

Work 3045 over chain stitches.

950

3808

3865

Work (1) 3045 over chain stitches.

3045

Work (4) 3045 over chain stitches.

310

# Christmas Botanical Ring Pillow | page 54

*DMC No. 25 embroidery floss: 543, 612, 839, 895, 919, 935, 936
*Use 2 strands, unless noted otherwise.
*The number in parentheses is the number of strands, followed by
the color code or name for the DMC No. 25 embroidery floss.

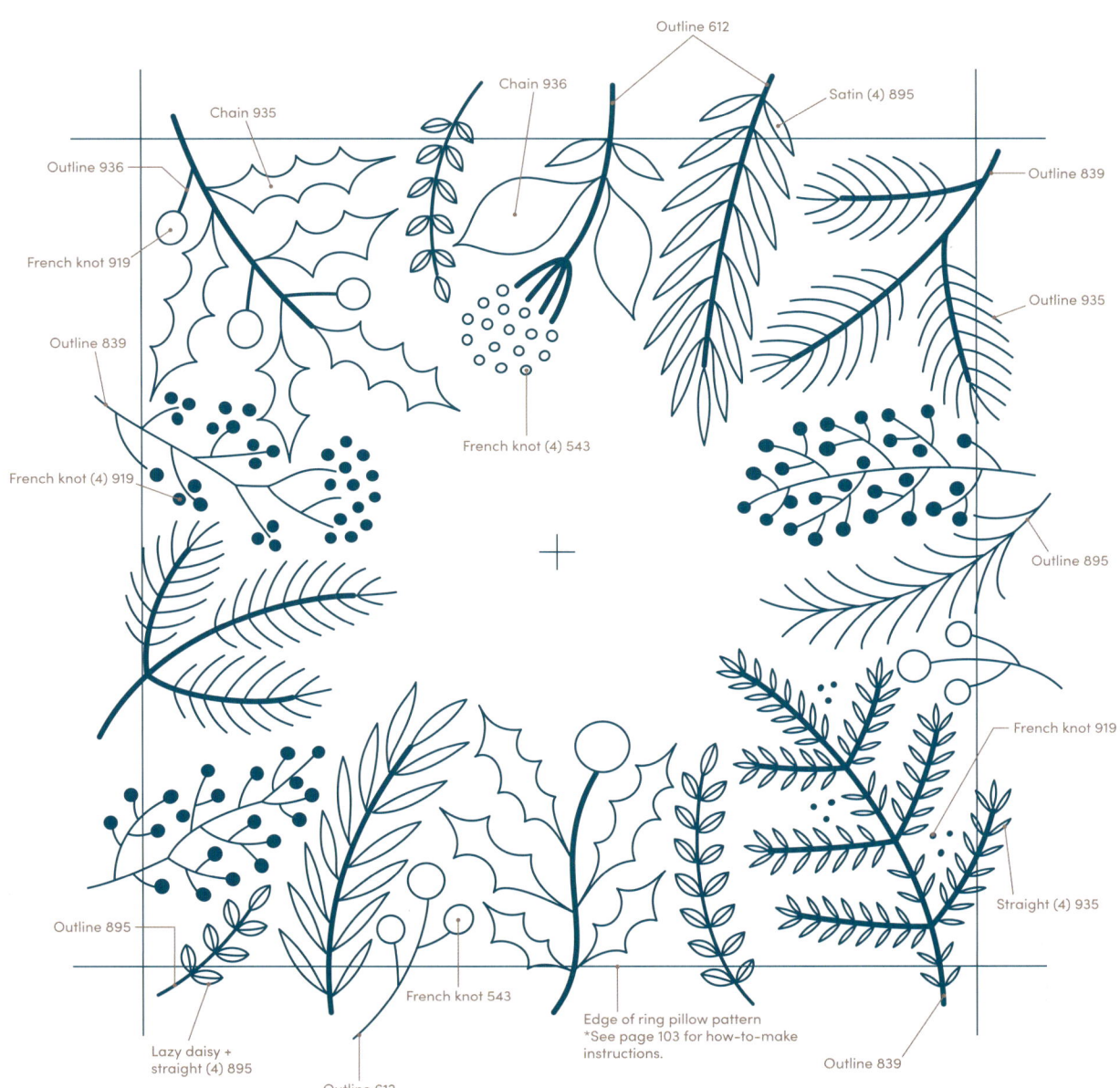

Outline 612

Chain 936

Chain 935

Satin (4) 895

Outline 936

Outline 839

French knot 919

Outline 935

Outline 839

French knot (4) 543

French knot (4) 919

Outline 895

French knot 919

Straight (4) 935

Outline 895

Lazy daisy +
straight (4) 895

French knot 543

Edge of ring pillow pattern
*See page 103 for how-to-make
instructions.

Outline 839

Outline 612

# Ornamental Embroidery Hoop (pages 7, 34, 55)

## MATERIALS

Exterior fabric: Embroidered work
Felt: Same dimensions as the embroidery hoop
Embroidery hoop: Sized to fit the project (page 7, 8¼" diameter; page 34, 5" diameter; page 55, 3¾" x 6½" oval)
Hand-sewing thread, same color as fabric, as needed

## HOW TO MAKE

1 Fit the embroidered fabric into the hoop, so that it's evenly balanced.
2 Turn over to the reverse side and cut the fabric in a circle (or oval), leaving approximately 2⅜"–2¾" from the edge. Use sewing thread to work running stitches approximately ½"–¾" from the edge, all the way around. Pull tightly on the thread to gather the fabric, and tie the thread with a French knot.
3 Cut the felt to a size that will hide the running stitches from step 2. Place over the reverse side of the hoop and whipstitch it in place all around.

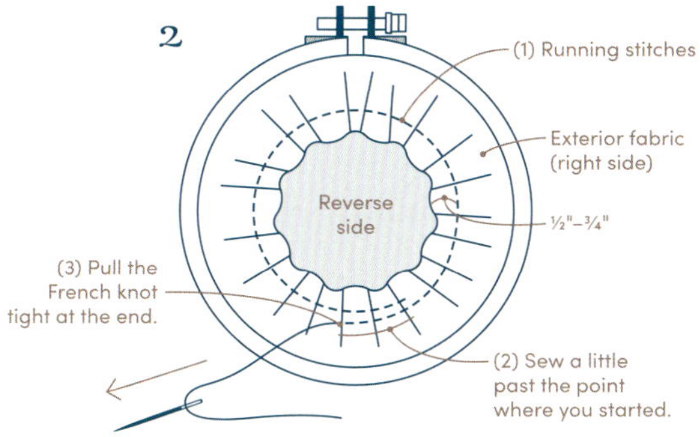

2
(1) Running stitches
Exterior fabric (right side)
Reverse side
½"–¾"
(3) Pull the French knot tight at the end.
(2) Sew a little past the point where you started.


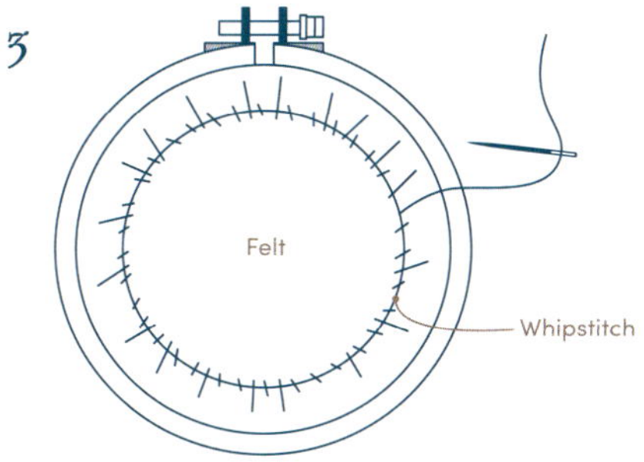

3
Felt
Whipstitch


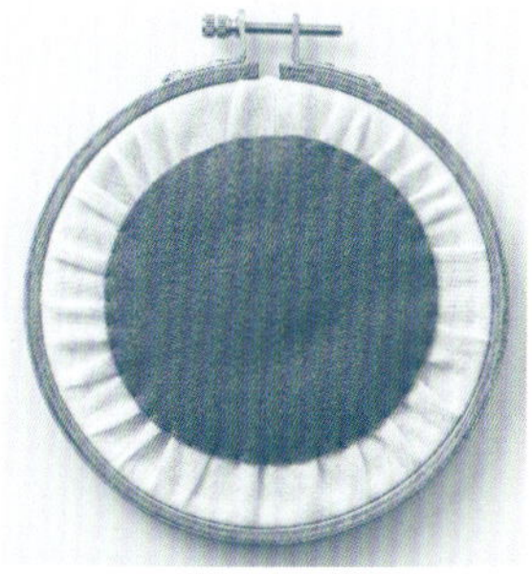

Finished project (reverse side)

# Violet Sachet (page 17)

Finished size: 3½" x 5¼"
DMC No. 25 embroidery floss: Refer to pattern on page 74.

## MATERIALS

Exterior fabric: Linen, black, 6" x 11¾"
⅛"-wide velvet ribbon, black, 15¾" long
Your choice of potpourri, as needed
Machine- or hand-sewing thread, same color as fabric, as needed

## HOW TO MAKE

1 Transfer the embroidery pattern (page 74) onto the right side of the exterior fabric, and trace lines for the pattern edges. Add basting stitches to mark the finished dimensions. Embroider the pattern, and iron your work lightly. Cut away excess fabric, adding approximately a ½" seam allowance all around.
2 Using an iron, press a ¼" triple fold at the top edge of the opening, and whipstitch in place with hand-sewing thread (you can also machine stitch in place). Repeat for the opposite end.
3 Fold the exterior fabric in half lengthwise, right sides out, sew the long sides together, a ¼" from the edge, and trim the seam allowances, leaving an ⅛".
4 Turn step 3 inside out, reshape, and sew the long sides together again, a ¼" from the edge. Take out the basting stitches, turn right side out, and lightly iron to reshape. Add whatever potpourri you like, and tie up the mouth of the bag with the ⅛"-wide velvet ribbon.

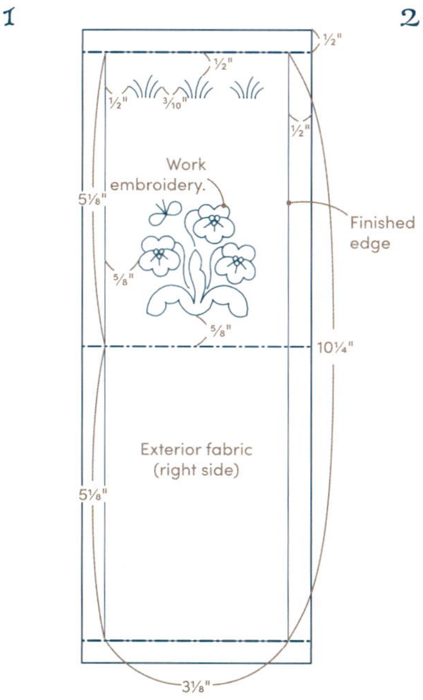

1
½"
½"
½"
³⁄₁₀"
½"
Work embroidery.
5⅛"
⅝"
⅝"
Finished edge
10¼"
Exterior fabric (right side)
5⅛"
3⅛"


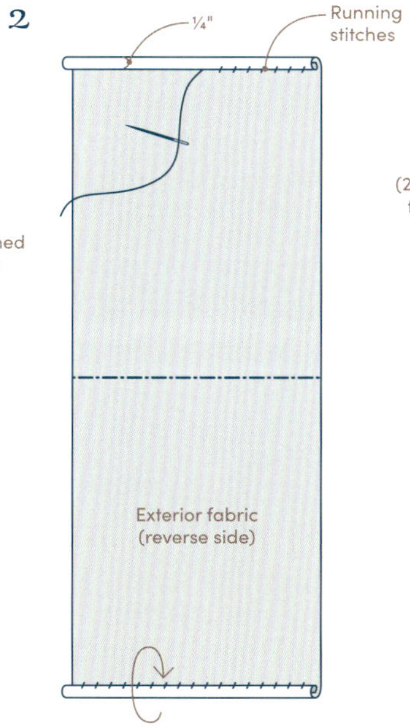

2
¼"
Running stitches
Exterior fabric (reverse side)


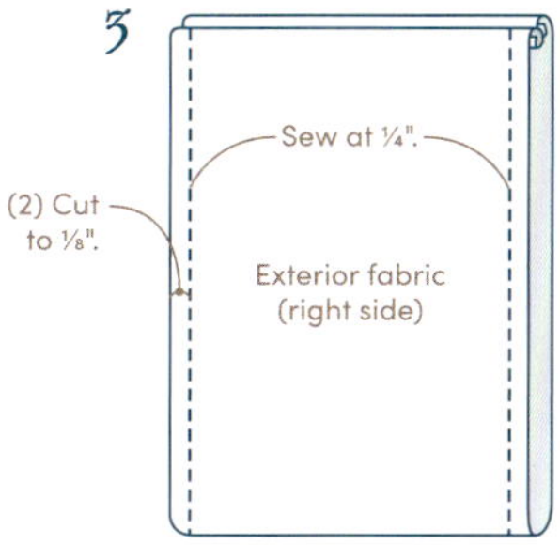

3
Sew at ¼".
(2) Cut to ⅛".
Exterior fabric (right side)


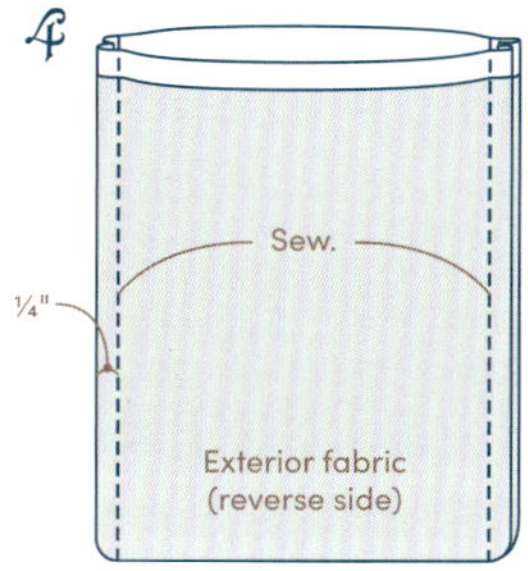

4
Sew.
¼"
Exterior fabric (reverse side)

# Koinobori (Carp Streamer) Tapestry (page 25)

Finished size: 15¾" x 7"
DMC No. 25 embroidery floss: Refer to pattern
   on page 82.

## MATERIALS

Exterior fabric: Linen, unbleached, 19¾" x 9¾", 2 pieces
¹⁄₁₆"-wide string, unbleached, 24" long, 2 pieces
Machine- or hand-sewing thread, same color as fabric,
   as needed

## HOW TO MAKE

1 Transfer the embroidery pattern (page 82) onto the
   right side of the exterior fabric, and trace lines for
   the pattern edges. Use basting stitches to mark the
   finished dimensions. Embroider the pattern, and
   iron your work lightly. Trim excess fabric, adding a
   ½" seam allowance all around.
2 Trace lines for the pattern edges on the reverse side
   of the second piece of the exterior fabric and cut in
   the same way as the exterior fabric from step 1.

3 Assemble the two pieces of exterior fabric,
   right sides together, with the two pieces of
   string each folded in half and sticking out
   from the upper sides, as shown, and sew
   together, leaving an opening for turning out.
4 Take out the basting stitches, turn right
   side out, and lightly iron to reshape. With
   a U-shaped ladder stitch, sew the opening
   closed.

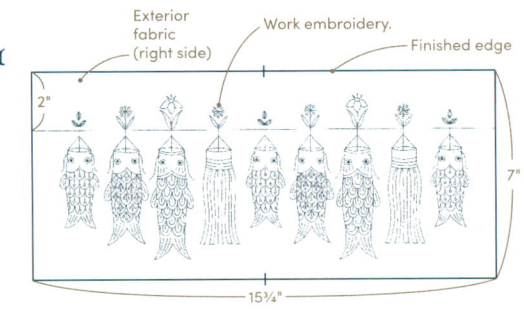
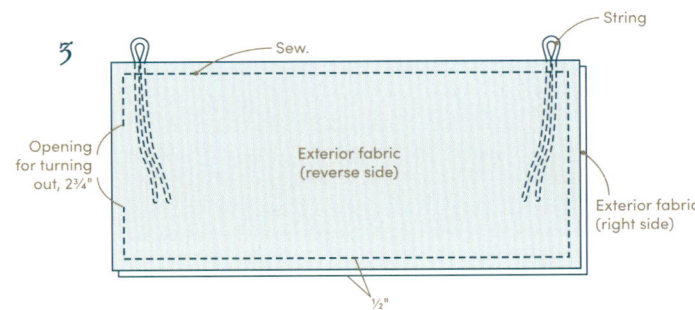

# Fabric Panel (pages 29, 46)

## MATERIALS

Exterior fabric: Embroidered work
Wood panel: Sized to fit the project (size used here,
   11¾" x 11¾")
Thumbtacks
Staple gun
Masking tape

## HOW TO MAKE

1 Lightly iron the embroidered fabric. Align the
   panel and the finished work, then trim excess
   fabric, leaving about 2" on all four sides of the
   panel.
2 Turn the fabric to the reverse side, set the panel
   on top, and use thumbtacks to hold the fabric
   in place evenly on all four sides. Once you've
   confirmed the position of the work, secure on
   all four sides with the staple gun, starting with
   the middle of each side and fastening alternate
   sides to prevent warping, leaving the corners
   open. As you work, make sure to check the
   position of the embroidery on the right side.

3 Fold up the corners of fabric, as shown, and
   secure with the staple gun.
4 Once you have secured everything, trim excess
   fabric. Use masking tape to hide the staples
   and create a smooth finish, which will also
   protect the wall if you hang it.

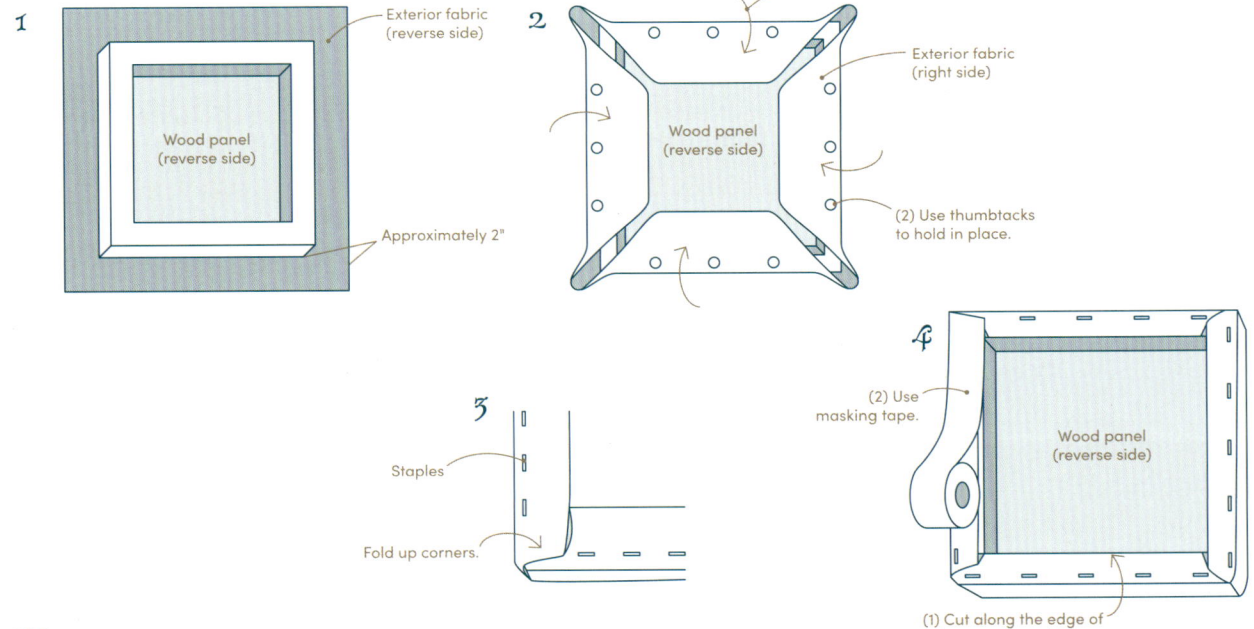

# Triangular Pot Holder (page 39)

Finished size: 4" x 4"
DMC No. 25 embroidery floss: 310, 349

## MATERIALS

Exterior fabric: Linen, gray, 9¾" x 6"
Lining fabric: Quilt cloth, unbleached, 9¾" x 9¾"
¹⁄₁₆"-wide linen string, 3½" long
Machine- or hand-sewing thread, same color as exterior
  fabric, as needed

## HOW TO MAKE

1 Transfer the lobster from the embroidery pattern on page 89 to the right side of the exterior fabric, as shown below, and trace lines for the pattern edges. Use basting stitches to mark the finished dimensions. Embroider the pattern, and iron your work lightly. Trim excess fabric, adding a ½" seam allowance all around.
2 Trace lines for the finished dimensions of the lining fabric and cut in the same way as the exterior fabric from step 1.
3 Assemble the exterior and the lining fabric, right sides together, and sew around the semicircular curve. Make cuts along the seam allowances.
4 Using an iron, press the seam allowances open, separating the exterior and lining fabrics and opening them out, then refold and align the seam.
5 Fold step 4 in half, with the string folded in half and inserted in between, [as shown,] and sew together, leaving an opening for turning out on the lining fabric. Take out the basting stitches, turn right side out, and lightly iron to reshape. With a U-shaped ladder stitch, sew the opening closed. Insert the lining fabric inside the exterior fabric.

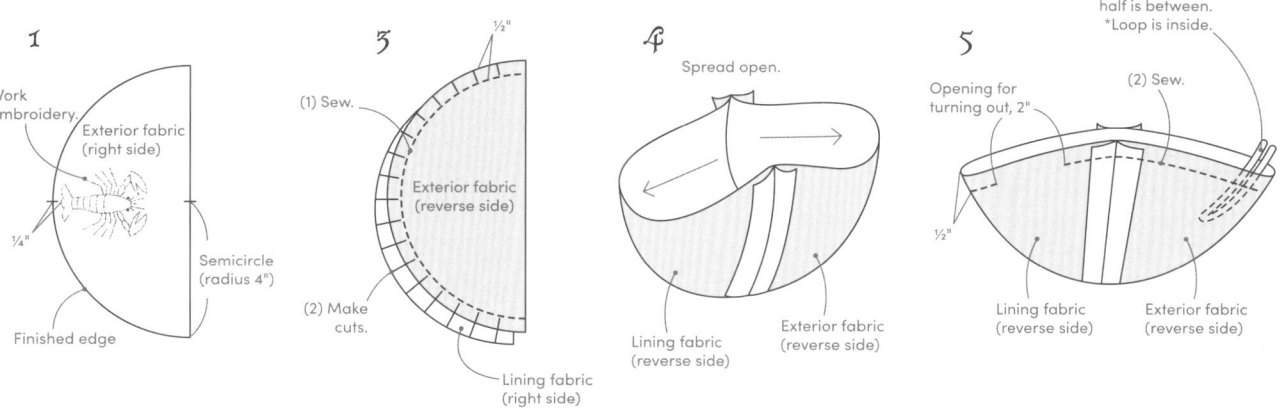

# Lesson Bag (page 43)

Finished size: 13⅜" x 15¾" (not including straps)
DMC No. 25 embroidery floss: ecru, 310, 610, 645

## MATERIALS

Exterior fabric: Linen, white, 15¾" x 35½"
Lining fabric: Linen, white, 15¾" x 35½"
Straps: Linen, white, 4" x 21¾", 2 pieces
Machine- or hand-sewing thread, same color as
  exterior fabric, as needed

## HOW TO MAKE

1 Transfer the embroidery pattern (page 103) onto the right side of the exterior fabric, and trace lines for the pattern edges. Use basting stitches to mark the finished dimensions. Embroider the pattern, and iron your work lightly. Trim excess fabric, adding a ½" seam allowance on all four sides.
2 Trace lines for the pattern edges of the lining fabric and cut in the same way as the exterior fabric from step 1.
3 Using an iron, press folds into the fabric for the handles as shown, and machine stitch both edges. Make two.
4 Fold the exterior fabric in half, right sides together, and sew both sides together. Press the seam allowances open. Repeat with the lining fabric, leaving an opening for turning out.
5 Assemble the exterior bag and interior bag from step 4 with right sides together, then insert the fabric for the handles from step 3 on each side, as shown, in between the exterior and interior bags, and sew all the way around the mouth of the bag.
  *You can reinforce where the handles are attached by backstitching several times.
6 Take out the basting stitches, turn right side out, and lightly iron to reshape. With a U-shaped ladder stitch, sew the opening closed.

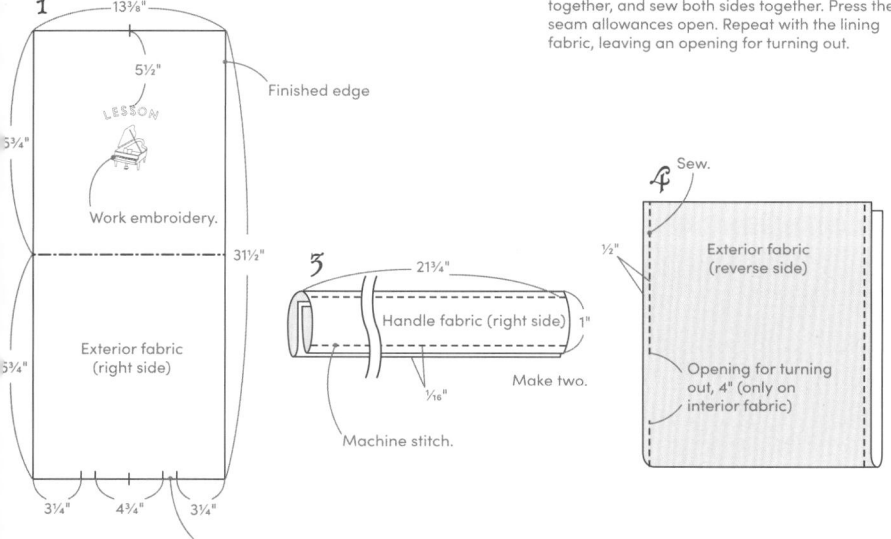

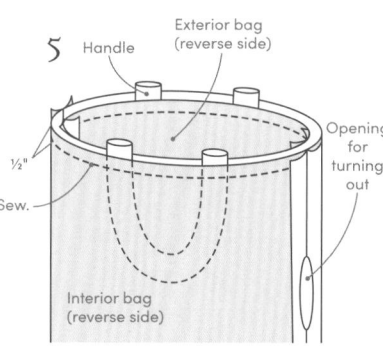

# Book Cover with Fallen Leaves (page 51)

Finished size: 12¼" x 6⅜"
DMC No. 25 embroidery floss: Refer to pattern
on page 92

## MATERIALS

Exterior fabric: Linen, dark gray, 17¾" x 9¾"
Lining fabric: Linen, unbleached, 17¾" x 9¾"
1¼"-wide ribbon, unbleached, 7⅞" long
Machine- or hand-sewing thread, same color as
exterior fabric, as needed

## HOW TO MAKE

1 Transfer the embroidery pattern (page 92) to
the right side of the exterior fabric, as shown
below, and trace lines for the pattern edges.
Use basting stitches to mark the finished
dimensions. Embroider the pattern, and iron
your work lightly. Trim excess fabric, adding a
½" seam allowance on all four sides. Trace lines
for the finished dimensions on the reverse side
of the lining fabric and cut in the same way.
2 Assemble the exterior fabric and lining fabric,
right sides together, and sew the edges
together on the pocket-flap side.

3 Fold the pocket flap inward, as shown, and
place the ribbon in between the fabrics at the
attachment mark. Sew together all around,
leaving an opening for turning out on the
pocket-flap side. Trim the seam allowances to a
¼" and make cuts at the corners.
4 Take out the basting stitches, turn right side out,
and lightly iron to reshape. With a U-shaped
ladder stitch, sew the opening closed.

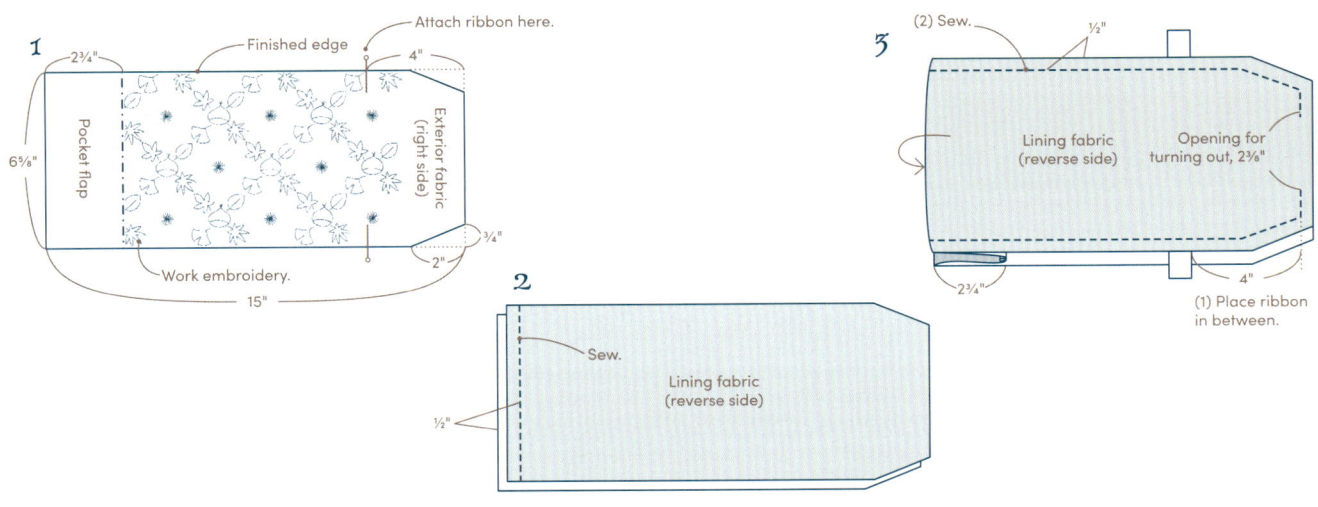

# Ribbon Brooch (page 54)

Finished size: 2¾" x 1½"
DMC No. 25 embroidery floss: Refer to pattern on
page 97

## MATERIALS (FOR ONE BROOCH)

Exterior fabric: Linen (A: cream / B: gray / C: red /
D: dark gray) 7⅞" x 4"
Center tie: Linen, same color as exterior fabric, 4" x 1¼"
Craft batting, as needed
Craft brooch pin (1)
Machine- or hand-sewing thread, same color as
exterior fabric, as needed

## HOW TO MAKE

1 Transfer the embroidery pattern (page 97) to
the right side of the exterior fabric, as shown
below, and trace lines for the pattern edges.
Use basting stitches to mark the finished
dimensions. Embroider the pattern, and iron
your work lightly. Trim excess fabric, adding a
½" seam allowance on all four sides.
2 Fold the center tie fabric into thirds, making a
½"-wide tie.
3 Fold back the seam allowances of both ends of
step 1 and match them up in the center, right
sides together, then pin them in place.

4 Sew the top and bottom edges together.
5 Take out the basting stitches, turn right side out
[from the center opening], reshape, and stuff
both ends with craft batting. With a U-shaped
ladder stitch, sew the opening closed.
6 Make gathers at the center, and wrap thread
around it. Wrap the center tie from step 2 twice
around the thread, sew in place on the reverse
side, and attach the brooch pin.

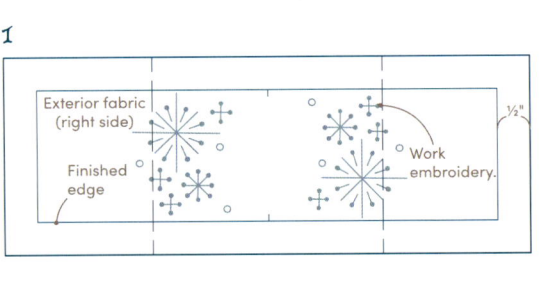

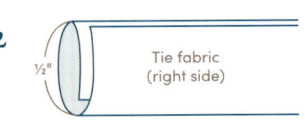

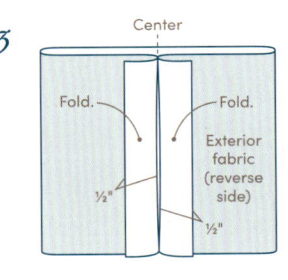

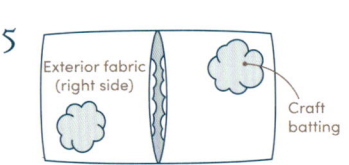

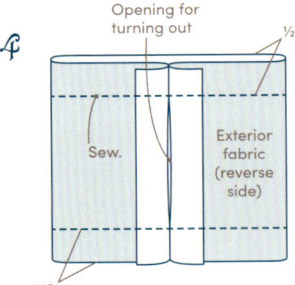

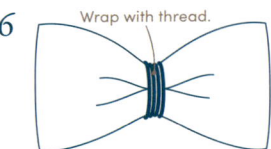

# Christmas Botanical Ring Pillow (page 54)

Finished size: 4¾" x 4¾"
DMC No. 25 embroidery floss: Refer to pattern on page 98.

## MATERIALS

Exterior fabric: Linen, white, 13¾" x 7⅞"
¼"-wide ribbon, red, 12¾" long
Craft batting, as needed
Machine- or hand-sewing thread, same color as exterior
fabric, as needed

## HOW TO MAKE

1 Transfer the embroidery pattern (page 98) to the right side of the exterior fabric, as shown below, and trace lines for the pattern edges. Use basting stitches to mark the finished dimensions. Embroider the pattern, and iron your work lightly. Trim excess fabric, adding a ½" seam allowance on all four sides.
2 Fold the fabric in half lengthwise, right sides together, and sew along the edge, leaving an opening for turning out.

3 Using an iron, press a crease on each side to center the seam from step 2, then sew the top and bottom edges together.
4 Take out the basting stitches, turn right side out, reshape, and stuff with craft batting. With a U-shaped ladder stitch, sew the opening closed. Fold the ribbon in half and sew it onto the middle of the cushion.

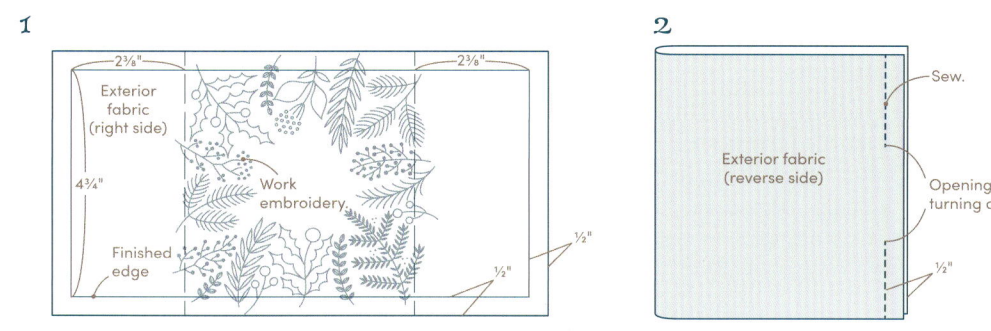
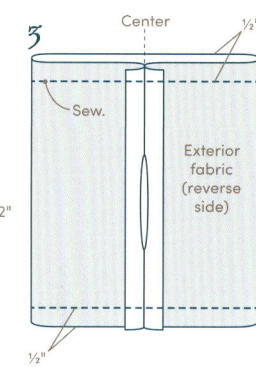

# Lesson Bag Pattern (page 101)

*See page 91 for how to embroider the piano.

Chain (2) 310
Work two rows.

## Yumiko Higuchi

After graduating from Tama Art University, Yumiko Higuchi worked as a handbag designer. Her pieces were shown and sold in boutiques. She began creating embroidery designs in 2008. She produces original embroidery patterns that feature botanical motifs and all manner of insects and living creatures.

Roost Books
An imprint of Shambhala Publications, Inc.
2129 13th Street
Boulder, Colorado 80302
www.roostbooks.com

Translation © 2025 by Shambhala Publications, Inc.
Translation by Allison Markin Powell
Originally published as *Kurashi no shishu* © 2023 by Yumiko Higuchi.

**BUNKA PUBLISHING BUREAU STAFF CREDITS**
Publisher: Takayoshi Seiki
Art Production & Book Design: Hiroaki Seki (Mr. Universe)
Photography: Yumiko Miyahama / Norifumi Fukuda (Bunka Publishing Bureau)
Styling: Kaori Maeda
Hair and Makeup: KOMAKI (nomadica)
Model: Audrey Kiddy (Sugar & Spice)
Cat: Marilyn (CAT LIVING Shelter Café)
Tracing & DTP: Yoshie Fujishiro
Proofreader: Masako Mukai
Editors: Mariko Tsuchiya (Three Season); Kaoru Tanaka (Bunka Publishing Bureau)

Parts of the Japanese edition of this book appeared in a series featured in *Misesu* magazine, from January 2020 to April 2021, forming the basis for these contents, which have been updated, expanded, and translated.

9 8 7 6 5 4 3 2 1

First English edition
Printed in China

Shambhala Publications makes every effort to print on acid-free, recycled paper. Shambhala Publications is distributed worldwide by Penguin Random House, Inc., and its subsidiaries.

ISBN: 978-1-64547-410-4
LC record available at https://lccn.loc.gov/2025940110

The authorized representative in the EU for product safety and compliance is eucomply OÜ, Pärnu mnt 139b-14, 11317 Tallinn, Estonia, hello@eucompliancepartner.com.